Spirit-Led Wealth

Spiritual Principles to Access Your Wealth Inheritance

Dr. Sonya R. Hamm

Spirit-Led Wealth

Spiritual Principles to Access Your Wealth Inheritance

Dr. Sonya R. Hamm

Unless otherwise indicated, Scripture quotations are from the authorized King James Version.

Scripture quotations marked (NKJV) are from the New King James Version. Copyright © 1982 by Thomas Nelson, Inc. Used by permission. All rights reserved.

Spirit-Led Wealth
"Spiritual Principles to Access Your Wealth Inheritance"
Copyright © 2015
Sonya R. Hamm

Some names and personal details have been change to protect the identity of those whose stories appear in this book.

Unless otherwise identified, Scripture quotations are from the HOLY BIBLE, KING JAMES VERSION® Copyright© 1973 by International Bible Society. Used by permission of Zondervan Publishing House. All rights reserved.

Scripture quotations identified AMP are taken from The Amplified Bible®, Copyright© The Lockman Foundation 1960. Used by permission.

Copyright © 1999, 2000, 2002, 2003 by Holman Bible Publishers, Nashville Tennessee. All rights reserved

All rights reserved. No part of this publication may be reproduced, stored in a retrieval system, or transmitted in any form or by any means – electronic, mechanical, photocopying, recording, or otherwise – without the prior written permission of the publisher and copyright owners.

ISBN: 978-1532723971
Printed in USA

DEDICATION

I dedicate this book to Father, Son and Holy Spirit. Our God is the God of All! I am thankful for the opportunity to pen this work with the purpose of helping as many people as possible build a loving and rewarding relationship with God through Jesus Christ.

To my husband Ronald and our children Brynique, Tynesia and Je'Ron—thank you for your love and support and the many sacrifices that you have each made. I give thanks for our adorable grandchildren Brycen, Jordynn, Mason and our new Lil Princess.

To the inPowerLife Church Family—thank you for your labor of love, support and prayers.

To the many mentors and friends who have added value to my life through your gifts and anointing.

My prayer is for this book to inspire the people of God to receive their wealth inheritance and reign in this life through Christ! Let continue to fund the Kingdom to ensure the gospel of Christ Jesus is preached from generation to generation.

Always Remember to:
Dream Big, Love Big, and Give Big!

TABLE OF CONTENTS

INTRODUCTION

Regardless of your current age or economic status the book you are holding in your hand promises to be a major influence in changing the rest of your life. Our Heavenly Father desires above all things that you prosper and be in health even as your soul prospers. You were created to live a life of health, wealth and abundance—there is no better time than now to make His desire your command. Our heavenly Father is looking for distribution centers –people He can trust to obey Him in the management and distribution of His wealth for the expansion of His Kingdom on the earth. Will you purpose in your heart to be one of the next Kingdom Expansion Financiers? If so, now is the time to "Access Your Wealth Inheritance" and begin the journey to your wealthy place in Christ.

One of the purposes of this book is to provide you with some timeless principles and promises from the Word of God. These principles will reveal His heart to you, strengthen your relationship with Him, and provide you with *Spiritual Principles to Access Your Wealth Inheritance.* Jesus clearly reveals in John 10:10 that his purpose for coming to the earth was to give us life and not just any life; but life *more* abundantly. Please allow this book to challenge your beliefs about wealth, renew your mind, and bring your heart into agreement with the will of God for your abundant life in Christ.

"Spirit-Led Wealth," speaks to the heart of how we should pursue and manage the wealth God entrusts with us. The Holy Spirit revealed to me through prayer, that our Heavenly Father is longing to see His children possess their *wealth inheritance* for the advancement of His kingdom on earth. I also saw the enemies' primary goal is to blind and block every Believer from possessing the wealth inheritance God has left to them.

Satan wants you to believe that God is against you desiring or having wealth. The purpose for satan's deception is to advance the kingdom of darkness with the wealth of the righteous. As long as Believers believe God does not want them to pursue and possess wealth they will never rise up and reign as *Kingdom Heirs* nor will they possess their wealth inheritance. The goal of this book is to help you expand your level of faith and believe for the seemingly impossible. "The things that are impossible with men are possible with God" **(Luke 17:27, emphasis added).**

With God on your side you can become a literal Millionaire or Billionaire—according to your faith. I believe that when you finish reading this book you will have enough faith and courage to pursue and live in your wealthy place. The first step is to embrace the truth that you are an **Heir of God**, who has been **Empowered Prosper**. Your heavenly Father has left you a **Wealth Inheritance** to be received and enjoyed right now—not after you die!

Altar calls are offered to set people free from various types of demonic influence. However, freedom from financial bondage is rarely offered, if ever. I believe the primary reason is financial freedom can only occur through systematic teaching. Scriptural teaching that can expose the deeply rooted lies of the enemy and the emotional baggage attached to them.

There are far too many Christians trapped by the devil's deceptions concerning wealth. They have been blinded to the truth that God desires for them to live abundant and prosperous lives. Allow this book to be your long awaited altar call for deliverance from financial oppression and lack into the possession of your wealth inheritance of abundance.

The time has come for the Body of Christ to be set free from financial bondage through *"Spirit-Led Wealth."* Open your heart and prepare your mind to receive *"Spiritual Principles to Access Your Wealth Inheritance."*

Chapter One

THE SOURCE OF ALL WEALTH

In the beginning God created the heaven and the
earth, (Genesis 1:1KJV).

Prayer requests flood the altar of churches around the globe every Sunday requesting God to meet financial needs. At the same time arguments continue to abound as to whether Christians should be wealthy. Americans and America are in greater debt than ever before and savings are at an all-time low. In addition, Christian divorces are at an all-time high with financial trouble as one of the primary causes. There are so many Christians living on the edge and one paycheck away from financial disaster. If you were to ask the average person what their greatest need is the response in most cases will be money.

Ho, every one that thirsteth, come ye to the waters, and he that hath no money; come ye, buy, and eat; yea, come, buy wine and milk without money and without price. Wherefore do ye spend money for that which is not bread and your labour for that which satisfieth not? (Isaiah 55:1-3 NKJV)

In the Scripture text above, God invites those who are in lack to come and buy from Him—without money and without price. He goes on to ask a question, **"Why do you spend money for that which is not food and your labor for that which cannot satisfy you?"** God is revealing how the Israelites were searching for fulfillment through things rather than a relationship with Him—much like society today. They were also working jobs that would never be able to adequately provide for nor satisfy their needs in the same way as He could.

The answer as to why financial turmoil has both Christians and non-Christians alike in bondage is because many have turned from God's way of doing things to following their own. The results speak for themselves. Through the influence of the enemy it is more difficult for Christians to recognize they have gone astray since they attend church, serve in ministry, pay tithes, pray, fast and so on. However, after all of the spiritual disciplines have been followed—money still seems to run out long before the month is over leaving most feeling powerless and hopeless.

In Isaiah 55:3, we find these instructions: **"Hearken diligently unto me, and eat ye that which is good, and let your soul delight itself in fatness.**

14

Incline your ear, and come unto me: hear, and your soul shall live; and I will make an everlasting covenant with you, even the sure mercies of David." I believe this is the cry of God's heart for the church today. He is calling His children to return and listen to Him and those who accept the invitation will eat food that is satisfying—our souls will live and we will delight in the fat (abundance) of the land. In other words, He is ready to blow our minds! God wants His children to stop the madness and turn from what they have created, to what *He* has prepared for us from before the foundation of the world.

First and foremost, God desires to have a loving relationship with you. Secondly, He wants to provide soul satisfying provision for you that will flow out of that relationship. Sounds like good news to me! God's thoughts about you are higher than your thoughts about yourself. His ways of blessing and prospering you are far greater than any plan you could ever dream of. He is ready to provide whatever you have the faith to dream for! It is not over! Right now, I challenge you to dream again!

The problem is too many of God's children are trying to reap spiritual blessings through the world's system of operation rather than the Kingdom of God's system. God did not create you to *"struggle, fake it, or barely make it!"* He wants to thoroughly provide for you in every area of your life. God has an economic strategy to prosper those who will obey Him and follow His way. In order for His plan to be revealed you have to transition from the world's way of thinking into Kingdom thinking and a principled life.

This book is designed to help you to *set your mind free!* You cannot keep the same mindset and expect things to change in your life—it simply will not happen. "You have to think new in order to create new, in your life." There must be a paradigm shift. You cannot use the same old mind that created a problem to change the problem (Albert Einstein).

In order to prosper God's way, it is important to possess the wisdom of God and understand His purpose for releasing wealth into the hands of His children. The Bible reveals in Psalms 111:10 that, "The fear of the LORD is the **beginning** of **wisdom**; a good understanding have all those who do His commandments. His praise endures forever." Fear in this case means to stand in awe or to humbly reverence someone as honorable or sovereign. Reverential fear is obtained the moment you become fully persuaded in your heart that, "In the beginning God created the heavens and the earth,"(Genesis 1:1) and understand that, "The earth is the Lord's and the fullness thereof, the world and all they that dwell therein,"(Psalm 24:1).

It is impossible to walk in humble reverence of someone else if you have not recognized their power, authority and ownership—their sovereign rule. If you understand and believe that God is the source of all power and He alone created and owns everything then you are walking in the fear of the Lord—the beginning of wisdom. Father God is the source of all wealth too!

Wisdom is the principal thing; therefore get wisdom: and with all thy getting get understanding. **Exalt her, and she shall promote thee:** she shall bring thee to honour, when thou dost embrace her, (Proverbs 4:7-8 NKJV).

Wisdom is the ability to understand how to properly execute knowledge to obtain a desired outcome. In short, wisdom knows how to do what and when to do it. It is not enough to have knowledge but you must understand how to properly apply that knowledge in your situation. To properly guide your financial affairs you need wisdom and true wisdom does not exist outside of God. In order for true wisdom to be released you have to have a relationship with God.

Suppose you have the combination to a safe holding millions of dollars—an inheritance left to you by your Father. Now, a perfect stranger walks up to you demanding that you give him the combination. Would you give it to him? Absolutely not! Why? Because you do not know him; there is no relationship in place that warrants you opening your treasure to him. You have no basis on which to trust this person. Our heavenly Father operates the same way. He is not going to open His treasure to strangers but only to those who are in relationship with Him—those He can trust to manage His affairs under His divine direction.

Who, then, is the man that fears the LORD? He will instruct him in the way chosen for him. He will spend his days in prosperity, and his descendants will inherit the land. The LORD confides in those who fear him; he makes his covenant known to them. (Psalm 25:13)

The Lord is patiently waiting on His children to return to Him and His system of operation. He wants to instruct them in the way He has chosen for them. The fear of the Lord is the beginning—recognizing that everything begins with, belongs to and ends in God. He is the source of all wealth, healing, power and life! The Scripture promises that the man who fears the Lord will be instructed by Him and he will spend his days in *prosperity* or dwell at ease and *his children will inherit the land.* (Psalms 25:13).

God has established a *covenant of blessing* for every believer. The only requirement to receive it is submission and obedience to His way of doing things. Psalm 25:14, makes it very clear that the secret of the Lord is revealed to them that fear Him. God will reveal His covenant and open His treasure to those who are in loving relationship with Him and make advancing His Kingdom a priority.

God is standing with His arms outstretched ready to impart to you the wisdom you need in order to move into your wealthy place. All you have to do is ASK! According to James 1:5-6: "If any of you lack wisdom, let him ask of God, that giveth to all men liberally, and upbraideth not; and it shall be given him. But let him ask in faith, nothing wavering. For he that wavereth is like a wave of the sea driven with the wind and tossed.

God's Word contains His covenant or His agreement to protect, prosper and promote those who are in right relationship with Him. Wisdom is the key to moving from your present condition into your wealthy place. God loves you and He wants you to live a fruitful and prosperous life.

CHAPTER TWO

EMPOWERED TO REIGN

It appalls me how so many Christians who proclaim to be the sons and daughters of God are still living defeated and oppressed lives. This is not the will of God. You and I serve the King of kings and the Lord of lords. You are a king under the King and a lord under the Lord. You have been given power and authority to rule in this life. The problem then is not with God but with man.

Take a moment to examine Romans 5:17:

"For if, by the trespass of the one man, death reigned through that one man, *how much more will those who receive God's abundant provision of grace and of the gift of righteousness* **reign in life through the one man, Jesus Christ,** (Romans 5:17 NKJV).

Do you see that! God has left an *abundant provision* of grace, or favor and the purpose is so that you can reign in this life. This *abundant provision* of grace is not automatically manifested—it has to be received.

The key point is that this abundant provision of grace is available for every believer.

The enemy has weaved a web of deception in the church causing many to believe they are not supposed to be wealthy. So many people subconsciously believe poverty keeps them humble. Wrong answer! Poverty prevents you from effectively reigning in the Kingdom of God and enjoying life.

To reign means to rule; to have royal or supreme power and to execute justice in a certain territory. Psalm 115:14-16 states, the Lord have given man the earth to reign or to rule in: "The Lord shall increase you more and more, you and your children. You are blessed of the Lord which made heaven and earth. Heaven, even the heavens, is the Lord's: **But the earth He hath He given to the children of men**. Okay, did you recognize the words increase and more and more? Friend, God has increase on His mind for you and your children. You are blessed (empowered) by God to prosper. So, why settle for less than what God desires for you?

The Lord has also given us dominion over the works of His hands: "What is man that You are mindful of him, and the son of [earthborn] man that You care for him? Yet You have made him but a little lower than God [or heavenly beings], and You have crowned him with glory and honor. **You made him to have dominion over the works of Your hands;** You have put all things under his feet: (Psalm 8:4-6 AMP). Can you imagine having dominion over the works of

God's hands? God has left you and me in charge to execute His plans and purposes in the earth realm.

Friend, you are royalty and as such you have been given authority to govern what enters and exits, not only in the earth realm, but also in your very life. Matthew 18:19 declares, that "Whatever you bind on earth shall be bound in heaven and whatever you loose on earth shall be loosed in heaven." This is the revelation that the enemy wants to keep hidden from the children of God. The devil does not mind you going to church or even praising God as long as he can keep you blind to your power and authority to rule. The devil does not want you to possess the wealth inheritance. Imagine, what would happen if every Believer was to arise right now and operate in their Kingdom authority—the devil's kingdom would be immediately destroyed. No wonder the enemy is working overtime to keep the children of God blind to their wealth inheritance and Kingdom authority.

Too many Believers are waiting on God to do something without realizing that He has already made the provision. The truth is God is waiting on you to take your rightful place as a *Kingdom Heir* and begin to *reign* in the earth realm.

But you are a chosen generation, a royal priesthood, a holy nation, His own special people, that you may proclaim the praises of Him who called you out of darkness into His marvelous light; who once were not a people but are now the people of God, who had not obtained mercy but now have obtained mercy, (1 Pet 2:9).

You are "*Royalty*" and your purpose is to be a walking display of the goodness of God, so others may be drawn out of darkness into His marvelous light. Would you want to listen to or follow someone that was in worse shape than you? No! Most people are looking for better. They desire a better life, a better position, a better whatever. I do not believe anyone is truly looking for less, although, they may have settled for less. I believe if more was offered to them and they believed they could obtain more they would accept more. Greater is offered to us through Christ!

There are men and women around you who will never come out of the prison of darkness and despair until you rise up and r*eign* in the territory that God has assigned to you. As a *Kingdom Heir* it is your responsibility to execute justice for the captives in your realm of influence. Confirmation is given in Romans 8:19-21, (AMP): **"For [even the whole] creation (all nature) waits expectantly and longs earnestly for God's sons to be made known [waits for the revealing, the disclosing of their sonship].** For the creation (nature) was subjected to frailty (to futility, condemned to frustration), not because of some intentional fault on its part, but by the will of Him who so subjected it--[yet] **with the hope that nature (creation) itself will be set free from its bondage to decay and corruption [and gain an entrance] into the glorious freedom of God's children.**

Every child of God needs to receive the revelation that God is waiting for them to possess their wealth inheritance and take their place as *Kingdom Heirs.* Why? Because the captives of the enemy are waiting on you to be revealed so that they can be set free. Think of it this way—the enemy will continue to keep your loved ones in bondage to the decay and corruption of the world until you rise up and help them gain entrance into the glorious freedom enjoyed by God's children. God wants you to take your place as a *Kingdom Heir,* receive your wealth inheritance and then help others to do the same.

The above referenced Scripture, not only points to the future revealing of the Sons of God, but the present revealing as well. Essentially there are two phases. The first phase occurred when you accepted Christ as your personal Lord and Savior. At that time you were adopted into the family of God. The second phase will occur at Christ's return—when the Believer will be raised incorruptible and forever changed.

In John 1:12 the Scripture reads, "But as many as received him, ***to them gave he power to become the sons of God,*** even to them that believe on his name." Now read that verse again, very slowly. I want you to see that salvation provides entrance into the Kingdom—with *power to become.* This indicates that the Believer must take some course of action after salvation. The promises, prophecies and principles contained in God's word are not automatic. They must be received and activated by faith. You have been given the *power to become!*

Jesus is seated at the right hand of the Father. Prior to His ascension He gave gifts unto men to continue His ministry on earth. God has called you to represent Him in the earth and He has given you ruler ship in the earth realm. Particularly, He has called you to rule in your sphere of influence—where you live! Someone's life depends on whether or not you will *access your wealth inheritance* and *reign* in this life.

1 Corinthians 5:18-20, (AMP) provides some key points about the Believer's new position and responsibility in Christ:

1. **The ministry of reconciliation has been transferred from Jesus and entrusted to the Believer—who is responsible to live a life that will compel others to be reconciled to God:** "But all things are from God, who through Jesus Christ reconciled us to Himself [received us into favor, brought us into harmony with Himself] **and gave to us the ministry of reconciliation [that by word and deed we might aim to bring others into harmony with Him].**

2. **The message of reconciliation has now been committed to the Believer—to teach men about the forgiveness, restoration and favor of God that is available to them:** "It was God [personally present] in Christ, reconciling and restoring the world to favor with Himself, not counting up and holding against [men] their

trespasses [but canceling them], and committing to us the message of reconciliation (of the restoration to favor).

3. **Lastly, the Believer is an Ambassador or personal representative of Christ—called to represent Him and God's Kingdom on the earth:** "So we are Christ's ambassadors, God making His appeal as it were through us. We [as Christ's personal representatives] beg you for His sake to lay hold of the divine favor [now offered you] and be reconciled to God.

You are an ambassador—called to represent Christ and execute God's authority in the earth realm. This is the assignment of every Believer not just a select few. I hear you saying, "But I'm not qualified." Oh, yes you are! Remember: you have been given the power to become the Son or Daughter of God.

God will never give you an assignment without providing you with the necessary provisions to fulfill it. You have been given the authority and power of Christ to *reign*, as stated by Christ Himself in Luke 10:19(AMP), **"Behold! I have given you authority and power** to trample upon serpents and scorpions, and [physical and mental strength and ability] **over all the power that the enemy [possesses]; and nothing shall in any way harm you.**

Well, God has left you to rule in the earth realm. You have been given full power to legislate (prepare and enact laws) in your realm of influence which means right now you can begin changing the very course of your life. Remember Matthew 18:19, "whatever you shall bind on earth shall be bound in heaven and whatever you shall loose on earth shall be loosed in heaven."

Furthermore, according to Ephesians 2:6 NKJV) God has, *"Raised us up together, and made us sit together in heavenly places in Christ Jesus:"*

You are seated in heavenly places as an Ambassador of Christ, called to, *"Advance the Kingdom of God on Earth."* I charge you therefore, to rise up and take your place as a *Kingdom Expansion Million-Heir* – begin r*eigning* in this life through Christ Jesus.

YOU HAVE BEEN EMPOWERED TO REIGN!

CHAPTER THREE

STOLEN IDENTITY

The original intent of God's heart was to create someone like Himself. He wanted a created being that He could give the dominion to rule and govern the territory of the earth. This is exemplified in Genesis 1:26-27, where God announces His desire and purpose for the creation of man, *"And God said, "Let Us make man in Our image, after Our likeness; and let them have dominion...over all the earth." So God created man in His own image, in the image of God created He him; male and female created He them."* God did not stop there; He went on in Genesis 1:28, to pronounce His blessing upon what He created, *"And God blessed them, and God said unto them, "Be fruitful and multiply, and replenish the earth, and subdue it; and have dominion...over every living thing that moveth upon the earth."* To bless means, that He empowered them with His favor, to accomplish His purpose on the earth.

I personally believe a lot of people unconsciously believe that God gave His blessing to Adam and Eve only. However, the blessing was pronounced in the Spirit realm, over all of humanity—not just to one man. The confusion exists because although God purposed and blessed humanity as a whole—the one man, who was Adam, forfeited the blessing through his disobedience. Adam's disobedience passed to all of humanity. However, Jesus Christ has paid the penalty and now humanity can be restored by placing faith in Him.

Take a look at Romans 5:12-16 (NKJV):

"Therefore, just as through one man sin entered the world, and death through sin, and thus death spread to all men, because all sinned— (For until the law sin was in the world, but sin is not imputed when there is no law. Nevertheless death reigned from Adam to Moses, even over those who had not sinned according to the likeness of the transgression of Adam, who is a type of Him who was to come.

But the free gift is not like the offense. For if by the one man's offense many died, much more the grace of God and the gift by the grace of the one Man, Jesus Christ, abounded too many. And the gift is not like that which came through the one who sinned. For the judgment, which came from one offense resulted in condemnation, but the free gift which came from many offenses resulted in justification.

All of humanity was affected by the fall of Adam. However, Jesus Christ is the doorway to reconciliation with God and the restoration of the Believer to God's favor and blessing. The enemy wants you to still believe you are under the curse invoked by Adam but the devil is a liar—you are free in Christ Jesus.

The main purpose of this book is to help you recognize and embrace the place of dominion, authority and prosperity you are supposed to occupy and operate in as a believer, in Christ. The same Word of blessing, multiplication and fruitfulness spoken by God in the beginning, still stands for your life today.

So, what exactly happened in the Garden? I submit that it was identity theft and highway robbery. The devil became angry after his jealousy of God and attempt to overthrow the throne of God caused him to be kicked out of heaven. The relationship, dominion and blessing that once belonged to him transferred to man. As a result, he became determined, that if he couldn't have it, neither would anyone else. Satan lied and deceived Adam and Eve, which is what, caused them to fall. Now he wants to deceive you as well.

Be sober, be vigilant, because your adversary the devil walketh about as a roaring lion, seeking whom he may devour, (1 Peter 5:8 NKJV).

The devil has not changed one bit. Today, he still seeks to introduce doubt, distort the self-image of man—and ultimately turn man's appetite from God to the world. The enemy's first line strategy is to cause you to doubt what God has said about you and promised to you. As I look around the Body of Christ, I must regretfully admit, that on the surface it looks like he is accomplishing his mission. Stop for a moment and think about how many people you know who are living in debt, defeat and despair—as born-again Believer's. The enemy is working overtime to keep you and those around you in darkness concerning your dominion and wealth inheritance.

The devil knows that you will never be able to produce more than you think you are worth; (*as a man thinks in his heart so is he*). Therefore, his job is to deceive you and entice you to move away from God's plan for your life. This attack of the enemy is aimed at your mind to cause your perception of God to change. In Malachi 3:6 God says, "I am the Lord, I change not..." This means that God is still the same loving, caring God who created you to have dominion and live a prosperous life. His love and promises can never change.

Adam and Eve relinquished the dominion, blessing and favor of God because the enemy deceived them to believe something different than what God said. As long as the devil can keep you in ignorance concerning your spiritual inheritance then he gains dominion and you remain defeated in that particular area of your life. Ultimately, the enemy's goal is to destroy the advancement of God's kingdom on the earth. He attempts to do this by blinding the Believer to the knowledge that they have dominion and a wealth inheritance. The saying, "What you don't know can't hurt you," is a lie straight from the pit of hell. What you don't know can destroy you and not only you but your children as well.

In Hosea 4:6 it is clear to see that God wants His children to obtain knowledge through Him and His Word, which is the weapon that will counterattack the deceptions of the enemy.

"My people are destroyed for lack of knowledge. Because thou hast rejected knowledge, I will also reject thee, that thou shalt be no priest to Me. Seeing thou hast forgotten the law of thy God, I will also forget thy children." (Hosea 4:6)

A few years ago my sister was the victim of identity theft. If she had not applied for a home mortgage loan she would have remained *ignorant* to the fact that someone had fraudulently acquired a very large sum of money in her name. During the investigation process my sister could not proceed with the purchase of her home. Due to the negative, unpaid balance on her credit report caused her desire to be delayed. There was also a possibility that she would be disqualified from the opportunity to purchase the home.

As I reflected on the situation plaguing my sister, I recognized that this was the exact strategy used by the enemy. He fraudulently steals the identity and wealth of the Believer without them even knowing it. Satan blinds the Believer to the promises of God through distractions.

The thief that stole my sister's identity was able to live in comfort and ease at her expense. The theft did not seem to affect my sister as long as she was unaware of its occurrence. However, behind the scenes her good name and credit was damaged. This is a very good example of how what we do not know can and does hurt us. My sister was blind to the fact that *an invisible enemy* was secretly destroying her identity, character and wealth. The devil is the invisible enemy who is doing the same exact thing in your life and the lives of so many other Believers.

Once my sister gained knowledge that she was robbed—she was able to take the appropriate action against the thief and have her identity and wealth restored. The thief was caught and ordered to repay all of the money. Now, it is your turn to take action against the thief that has been robbing you.

The Scripture teaches that a thief must repay seven times what he stole even if it means turning over his entire household. "Men do not despise a thief if he steals to satisfy himself when he is hungry; **But if he is found out, he must restore seven times [what he stole]; he must give the whole substance of his house [if necessary--to meet his fine]** (Proverbs 6:30-31 AMP).

I serve notice to you that the devil, who is the thief, has been caught by the Blood of the Lamb! Jesus has ordered the thief to restore to you seven times what he has stolen from you. Not only you, but all of those who are connected to you. Friend it is time to re-claim your identity and possess your *wealth inheritance!*

...For the devil has sinned (violated the divine law) from the beginning. **The reason the Son of God was made manifest (visible) was to undo (destroy, loosen, and dissolve) the works the devil [has done]** (1 John 3:8).

Jesus has destroyed the works of the devil. Yet, there are a lot of brothers and sisters in Christ, who are blind and being robbed through a lack of knowledge. Their identities and wealth have been stolen—they are blind to the knowledge that an invisible enemy is destroying them. I want to help them catch the thief and receive the seven-fold return in their life.

God has placed a desire in my heart to reach at least one million people with the message contained in this book. I am so glad that you are one of the *one million*. I am sure you want to make your friends and loved ones aware of the invisible enemy—who is destroying and robbing them of their wealth inheritance.

IT IS TIME TO RECOVER ALL!

Chapter Four

THE WEALTH COVENANT

God is a God of covenant. The word covenant means, a solemn agreement or promise made between two people. God has established a solemn agreement with those who place their faith in Jesus Christ. The promises, contained in the Covenant of God, are available to every born-again Believer. Again, I must remind you that the promises of God do not automatically manifest in your life—they must be activated by faith. God's covenant promises have been established forever and cannot be changed or annulled. However, you can forfeit the benefits of His promises through ignorance of their existence or disobedience to God's established order.

For when God made a promise to Abraham, because He could swear by no one greater, He swore by Himself, saying, "Surely blessing I will bless you, and multiplying I will multiply you." (Hebrews 6:13-14, KJV).

Now, I want you to stop and meditate on the above passage for a few moments. Notice, that when God makes a promise He swears by Himself. There is no one greater than Him to swear by—He is the creator of all things that exist. Therefore, the authority to bless and multiply His creation begins and ends in Him. His promise of what He will do is His word that it is already done. God did not ask Abraham whether or not he wanted to be blessed. In the same way God is not asking you—He has already given His word that He will bless and multiply you.

God made a covenant or agreement with Abraham during a time when both Abraham and Sarah's bodily strength was incapable of producing. Romans 4:19-21 reads; *"And being not weak in faith, he considered not his own body now dead, when he was about a hundred years old, nor yet the deadness of Sarah's womb. He staggered not at the promise of God through unbelief, but was strong in faith, giving glory to God, and being fully persuaded that what He had promised, He was able also to perform."* Friend, God is not dependent on your ability or strength to bring what He has promised you to pass in any way. The only thing you have to do is agree with His word which is already settled in heaven. You may be in a hopeless situation right now—"But God!"

Wow! Can you feel the chains being loosed from your heart and mind? The only thing Abraham had to work with was his faith. In the same way, all God needs from you, is your faith in His ability to perform what He has promised. So many people are waiting for some secret code to be revealed on how to become wealthy. There is no secret code—just simple faith in God and His plan to bless and prosper you.

The Word of God, as found in Hebrews 6:13-20, serves as a great example of God's covenant with Abraham and the *heirs* of promise (you). It also reveals His inability and unwillingness to break His oath. I encourage you to stop right here. Allow this passage of Scripture to minister to your spirit before moving to the next chapter. I want you to see that God's Covenant to bless and multiply you is absolutely irreversible.

For when God made [His] promise to Abraham, He swore by Himself, since He had no one greater by whom to swear, Saying, Blessing I certainly will bless you and multiplying I will multiply you. And so it was that he [Abraham], having waited long and endured patiently, realized and obtained [in the birth of Isaac as a pledge of what was to come] what God had promised him. Men indeed swear by a greater [than themselves], and with them in all disputes the oath taken for confirmation is final [ending strife].

Accordingly God also, in His desire to show more convincingly **and beyond doubt to those who were to inherit the promise** the unchangeableness of His purpose and plan, intervened (mediated) with an oath. This was so that, by two unchangeable things [His promise and His oath] in which it is impossible for God ever to prove false or deceive us, we who have fled [to Him] for refuge might have mighty indwelling strength and strong encouragement to grasp and hold fast the hope appointed for us and set before [us]. [Now] we have this [hope] as a sure and steadfast anchor of the soul [**it cannot slip and it cannot break down under whoever steps out upon it**--a hope] that reaches farther and enters into [the very certainty of the Presence] within the veil, where Jesus has entered in for us [in advance], a Forerunner having become a High Priest forever after the order (with the rank) of Melchizedek. (Hebrews 6:13-20 AMP)

The same promise God made to Abraham is still in effect and available to you today. The plans and purposes of God are unchangeable and it is impossible for Him to deceive you. He has sealed His promises with an oath. It is so important that you understand God's inability to lie or change. Otherwise, you will always believe that you have to do something to earn God's blessing. God's covenant promises are released to you by faith—not by works. In John 6:28-29, Jesus was ministering and the people asked Him a question: "Then they said to Him, "What shall we do, that we may work the works of God?" Jesus answered and said to them, "This is the work of God that you believe in Him whom He sent." The same answer applies to you my friend. God only requires you to believe His Son who is the Word.

Take a moment and reflect upon God. Stretch out your arms and receive His love and concern for you. It is very important that you embrace the love of God before you continue reading. God's love for you will serve as the guiding force that enables you to receive the abundant life He has prepared for you. Faith works by love and you cannot place your faith in someone that you do not love or believe loves you.

Now, you can step out in full assurance of faith that what God has promised, He is also able to perform. It does not matter where you are or what your present condition is. If you have accepted Jesus Christ as your Lord and Savior you are qualified. The promises contained in God's covenant are available for you to receive by faith.

In order to lay claim to your wealth inheritance you first need to be persuaded that you have one. Let us journey on and I will show you that your *wealth inheritance* is available for you to possess today—not when you get to heaven.

ACCEPT GOD'S COVENANT OF WEALTH!

CHAPTER FIVE

DELIVERED INHERITANCE

Have you ever secretly wished you would get a phone call or someone would knock on your door and inform you a wealthy relative has died and you were named as the heir of his estate? Well, today I have some good news for you! A wealthy relative has died, His Estate has been settled, and you have been named as an *heir*. His estate is so abundant and full of riches that not only were *you* named heir, but everyone who will believe on Him in faith is an heir too. Isn't this awesome! The wealthy relative is Jesus Christ!

The Spirit Himself [thus] testifies together with our own spirit, [assuring us] that we are children of God. And if we are [His] children, then we are [His] heirs also: heirs of God and fellow heirs with Christ [sharing His inheritance with Him]; only we must share His suffering if we are to share in His glory. (Romans 5:16-17 AMP)

Dearly beloved, you are an heir of God and joint-heir with Jesus Christ! Jesus Christ has left us all an inheritance. The word *heir* means a successor or beneficiary of property. In the case of Christ, we have become both the successor and the beneficiary of His property. You have a legal right to take possession.

But Jesus has now obtained a superior ministry, and to that degree He is the mediator of a better covenant, **which has been legally enacted on better promises**. (Hebrews 8:6 AMP)

The covenant, and promises contained therein have been made better through the sacrifice of Jesus Christ. God's desire is for you to receive the fulfillment of what He has left you. Take note of the fact that the inheritance is everlasting. Your inheritance is available for you to possess right now!

[Christ, the Messiah] is therefore the Negotiator and Mediator of an [entirely] new agreement (testament, covenant), **so that those who are called and offered it may receive the fulfillment of the promised everlasting inheritance--since a death has taken place which rescues and delivers and redeems them from the transgressions committed under the [old] first agreement** (Hebrew 9:15 AMP).

For where there is a [last] will and testament involved, the death of the one who made it must be established, **for a will and testament is valid and takes effect only at death, since it has no force or legal power as long as the one who made it is alive** (Heb. 9:16-17 AMP).

The death of Jesus Christ has been established therefore, His last will and testament is now in effect. Due to the fact you accepted Jesus as your personal Lord and Savior; you were named as an *heir* to His estate. You have an inheritance that includes more than salvation and forgiveness from sin. This inheritance entitles you to access and possess everything that God the Father and His Son Jesus owns. Can you stop and shout right there! .

The following Scriptures serve to further reveal your inheritance in Christ:

1. ...to open their eyes, and to turn them from darkness to light, and from the power of Satan unto God, that they may receive forgiveness of sins, *and inheritance* among them which are sanctified by faith that is in me, (Acts 26:18 KJV).

2. In whom also **we have obtained an inheritance**, being predestinated according to the purpose of him who worketh all things after the counsel of his own will, (Ephesians 1:11 KJV).

Jesus' death not only paid the penalty of your sin, but it also unlocked your destiny and released your inheritance which includes wealth. In Acts 26:18, you can clearly see a distinction has been made between the forgiveness of sins and the inheritance. A lot of teaching has gone forth on the forgiveness of sins and the inheritance of eternal life. There has not been enough teaching on the portion of the inheritance that we are to possess in this life concerning our wealth.

3. And now, brethren, I commend you to God, and **to the word of his grace, which is able to build you up, and to give you an inheritance** among all them which are sanctified (Acts 20:32).

God's Word, which contains His covenant promises, is what builds you up to receive your inheritance. The more time you spend in the Word of God the stronger your faith becomes. The stronger your faith becomes the more relentless you will become in claiming the promises, prophecies and principles of God into your life. The Word of God is God's will concerning what you can be, do and have in this life and the life to come.

Can you see why the devil doesn't want you to read your Bible (Covenant)? The enemy wants to keep you blind to your wealth inheritance so he can continue to advance his kingdom of darkness with your stuff!

4. ...knowing that from the Lord you will receive **the reward of the inheritance;** for you serve the Lord Christ, (Colossians 3:24KJV).

The reward for serving Jesus is your inheritance. I am so glad you decided to follow Jesus!

5. Blessed be the God and Father of our Lord Jesus Christ, which according to his abundant mercy hath begotten us again unto a lively hope by the resurrection of Jesus Christ from the

dead, **to an inheritance incorruptible, and undefiled, and that fadeth not away, reserved in heaven for you** (1 Peter 1:4 NKJV).

Your inheritance is incorruptible – it cannot be destroyed, it is undefiled – pure, it will not fade away—*it is reserved in heaven,* right now waiting for you to claim it. It does not matter how old you are nor what your present condition is. There is a reservation in heaven waiting for you to claim and it is your wealth inheritance. Come on! Confirm your reservation and claim your inheritance in Jesus Name!

Our heavenly Father is not crooked, broke, cheap or selfish. He is not sitting in heaven with His back turned to you, nor is He angry with you. He is, however; waiting on you to claim what rightfully belongs to you—Your Wealth Inheritance! All you have to do is receive it. Read Matthew 7:7-11 NKJV:

"Ask, and it will be given to you; seek, and you will find; knock, and it will be opened to you. For everyone who asks receives, and he who seeks finds, and to him who knocks it will be opened. Or what man is there among you who, if his son asks for bread, will give him a stone? Or if he asks for a fish, will he give him a serpent? If you then, being evil, know how to give good gifts to your children, how much more will your Father who is in heaven give good things to those who ask Him!

Friend I hope you understand in your spirit that your heavenly Father wants to give you good things. God is not taking from you and He has not destined you to live a life of *struggling, faking it, and barely making it.*

47

It is time to declare war with the real robber—the devil! Are you tired of trying to make it all by yourself in your own strength? Are you tired of living a mediocre, unfulfilled, broke life? Are you tired of being robbed by the devil? If the answer is yes to any of the above questions please stand right where you are and declare war on the devil. Declare war on the devil by announcing the following statement to him: "I announce to every demonic force that you will never steal from me another day in my life—I recognize that I am an heir and I have been left an inheritance. I command you satan in the name of Jesus to begin returning everything you have stolen, right now!

Remember; the Word says the thief has to return seven times what He has stolen. Let him know you receive your wealth inheritance now and command him to restore seven-fold in Jesus Name!

If you think you're blessed right now read on because there are more schemes the enemy has used to keep you blind. I want to help you uncover these schemes as well as impart more revelation to you from the Word of God concerning your wealth inheritance. I am determined to help you get it all back!

Chapter Six

THE GREAT WEALTH TRANSFER

One Saturday evening I was driving from Austin, Texas after a real-estate course when all of sudden my trip was interrupted by the presence of God. As I continued to drive, I distinctly heard the Spirit of God say, "Sonya, I did not create my people to live on credit or in debt. Debt belongs to the world's system of operation." "I created my people to live an abundant life; full of good things".

He then instructed me to search His Word and study how wealth was transferred from one generation to the next. I was shocked at what the Holy Spirit revealed to me through that study. I found that the Bible was full of people who had great wealth and the best part of it all was God blessed them with it. I then began to realize that my perspective of God in relation to wealth was totally warped and it wasn't based so much on what I learned from the world, but rather what I had learned at Church. To my dismay, after years of study I learned that what the Church had taught, or didn't teach, about wealth was in total error to what I was now learning from the Word of God. Please understand that I am only speaking in reference to some churches I attended in my formative years. I later realized that there were many churches teaching on prosperity—I just was not aware of them.

In this chapter I want to share with you some highlights of what I've learned about wealth and how it was transferred from one generation to the next, right down to you and I. I pray that you open your heart because in order to move into your wealthy place you have to believe that it is the will of God for you to live a life of abundance. Here is "A Biblical Portrait of the Great Wealth Transfer," designed to help you see how God blessed and prospered others, and how He wants to transfer that blessing to you and the generations after you. I want to systematically show you how the wealth of the forefathers has transferred to you.

First, the death of Jesus on the cross delivered us from the curse of poverty, sickness and death.

Christ redeemed us from the curse of the law, having become a curse for us; for it is written, Cursed is every one that hangeth on a tree: (Galatians 3:13 NKJV).

Bless the LORD, O my soul; and all that is within me, bless His holy name! Bless the LORD, O my soul, and forget not all His benefits-- **who forgiveth all thine iniquities, who healeth all thy diseases, who redeemeth thy life from destruction, who crowneth**

thee with lovingkindness and tender mercies, who satisfieth thy mouth with good things, so that thy youth is renewed like the eagle's. The LORD executeth righteousness and judgment for all that are oppressed (Psalms 105:1-6 NKJV).

Do you see the benefits package delivered to you through your faith in Jesus Christ! I encourage you to rehearse your benefits out loud every day until you memorize it. This is a powerful tool to use against the enemy when he attempts to plague you with disease or tries to bring destruction in your life. The Word of God is powerful and a sure defense!

Second, the purpose of Jesus breaking the curse was so that the blessing of Abraham could come upon the Gentiles (You and me).

To the end that through [their receiving] Christ Jesus, **the blessing [promised] to Abraham might come upon the Gentiles,** so that we through faith might [all] receive [the realization of] the promise of the [Holy] Spirit, (Galatians 3:14 AMP).

After reading this I could not help but wonder what blessings were promised to Abraham. Well guess what? I found the answer and so much more. I really like this passage in the Amplified Bible because it gives so much clarity to the Scripture and helps you relate to it from a personal perspective.

NOW [in Haran] the Lord said to Abram, Go for yourself [for your own advantage] away from your country, from your relatives and your father's house, to the land that I will show you, (Genesis 12:1 AMP).

God interrupted Abrams life and gave him instructions to leave everything familiar to him—much like He did me the evening I was in the car and He spoke to me. I believe this is exactly what God is doing with you as you read this book. He wants you to let go of everything familiar to you, all of the old teaching and beliefs about money and He wants you to allow the Holy Spirit to lead you into your wealthy place. Just as He had a plan for Abraham; He also has a plan for you.

And I will make of you a great nation, and I will bless you [with abundant increase of favors] and make your name famous and distinguished, and you will be a blessing [dispensing good to others] Genesis 12:2 AMP).

"And I will bless those who bless you [who confer prosperity or happiness upon you] and curse him who curses or uses insolent language toward you; in you will all the families and kindred of the earth be blessed [and by you they will bless themselves"(Gen. 12:3 AMP).

Look at the covenant promise you have access to through your faith in Jesus. Everything God promised Abraham is transferred to you. Now, let's examine these scriptures from a prophetic viewpoint and how they relate to us today.

God promises Abram that He is going to make Him a great nation. The word nation speaks of a group of people who have common descent, language or

52

culture and who are governed under one government. So, God is saying to you that based on your obedience to Him and what you teach those connected to you, a great nation will be formed out of you. This speaks to the future of your children, their children, and so on. Secondly, God promises to bless you with abundant increase of favors and make your name great. Right now you might be broke as a joke with bad credit, but not for long. When you have the favor and blessing of God you really do not need money or earthly credit to receive your wealth inheritance. Did you get that! You don't need money or credit! I want you to get your mind off of more money or better credit. That will come once you build yourself up spiritually.

God promises to bless you with abundance and make your name great. The day you made Jesus the Lord of your life your name became great. *If any man be in Christ he is a new creation old things are passed away and all things have become new* (2 Cor. 5:17 KJV). Everything concerning you is new and now you have the power to begin calling those things that are not (in your life) as though they are, in Christ. Now, if you have bad credit, you need to correct it so that your earthly record reflects your heavenly one. You do not have to be bound by your credit or lack of money since God has thousands of ways to bless you.

One of the reasons God wants to bless you is so you can be a blessing to others. Understand this: God and Jesus are both in heaven and you have been left here on earth to execute the business of the Kingdom until Jesus returns. Jesus has given you power of attorney to legally act in His name and under His authority. The devil is on a mission to keep you blind to this truth so that he can continue propagating his lies and blocking the progress of God's kingdom on earth. You have been called to bless (empower) others by teaching them God's plan so they can be set free from the devil's lies, unlock their wealth inheritance, and join the *"Spirit-Led Wealth Movement* to *Advance the Kingdom of God on the Earth.*

God is committed to blessing those who bless you. Those who curse you will themselves be cursed. I am glad to be one of the ones' sent to bless you! Those who commit to helping you in your kingdom assignment will receive favor from God in their life, "Knowing that whatsoever good thing any man doeth, **the same shall he receive from the Lord**, whether he be bond or free, (Ephesians 6:8 KJV). Likewise, you become a partaker of the anointing and blessing on the life of all those that you bless, *"And in the defense and confirmation of the gospel, ye all are partakers of my grace,* (Philippians 1:7 KJV).

I feel sorry for all the people who have rejected you or cursed you because in reality they have hurt themselves. Friend, you are very important in the plan of God and He is waiting on you to recognize that *Somebody's life depends on you.* The last portion of Genesis 12:3 declares that in Abram (You), all the families of the earth will be blessed. This promise began with Abraham but it did not end with him. It was transferred to Isaac, Jacob and now to you! The future generations of your family will be blessed by you when you put into action the things you learn in this book.

And the "Scripture, foreseeing that God would justify (declare righteous, put in right standing with Himself) the Gentiles in consequence of faith, proclaimed the Gospel [foretelling the glad tidings of a Savior long beforehand] to Abraham in the promise, saying, in you shall all the nations [of the earth] be blessed, (Galatians 3:8 AMP).

"And Abram was very rich in cattle, in silver, and in gold."(Genesis 13:2 KJV)

Based on the above scripture, it is clear that God chose a wealthy man to establish His covenant; not someone who was broke. God does not have a problem with His children having wealth as Abraham was wealthy. God is a God of abundance; therefore, I believe He chose someone who was like Him – Abundant! Abraham not only committed himself to God but he committed everything he owned. It has always been the heart of God to bless and multiply His children; therefore, Abraham serves as a role model of how every believer can and should seek to live— abundantly, prosperously, blessed!

The Covenant God made with Abraham was transferred to Isaac:

And there was a famine in the land, beside the first famine that was in the days of Abraham. And Isaac went unto Abimelech king of the Philistines unto Gerar. And the LORD appeared unto him, and said,

Go not down into Egypt; dwell in the land which I shall tell thee of: Sojourn in this land, and I will be with thee, and will bless thee; for unto thee, and unto thy seed, I will give all these countries, **and I will perform the oath which I swore unto Abraham thy father;** And I will make thy seed to multiply as the stars of heaven, and will give unto thy seed all these countries; and in thy seed shall all the nations of the earth be blessed; **Because that Abraham obeyed my voice, and kept my charge, my commandments, my statutes, and my laws** (Genesis 26:1-5 KJV).

God's covenant promises are so powerful that even in the midst of adversity He causes His people to continue to prosper. Isaac understood the power of a seed and when he sowed *(in a time of famine)* he prospered and became very rich. Isaac received a hundred times more than what he planted, *in the same year*! Read and meditate on Genesis 26:12-14:

Then Isaac sowed seed in that land and received in the same year a hundred times as much as he had planted, and the Lord favored him with blessings. **And the man became great and gained more and more until he became very wealthy and distinguished;** he owned flocks, herds, and a great supply of servants, and the Philistines envied him.

Let me give you a word of warning: when you really grab hold of this revelation and the blessings of God begin to manifest in your life, people are going to envy you just as the Philistines envied Isaac. They could not understand how he was prospering in the midst of a famine. People are not going to understand you! What a mighty God we serve!

Abraham lived a lifestyle of obedience and worship to the Father and he taught Isaac how to be in relationship with God. As a result, God's covenant of wealth transferred from Abraham to Isaac.

The Covenant transfers from Isaac to his son Jacob prior to his death:

Then his father Isaac said to him, "Come near now and kiss me, my son." And he came near and kissed him; and he smelled the smell of his clothing, and blessed him and said: "Surely, the smell of my son is like the smell of a field which the LORD has blessed. Therefore may God give you of the dew of heaven, of the fatness of the earth, and plenty of grain and wine. Let peoples serve you, and nations bow down to you, be master over your brethren, and let your mother's son's bow down to you. **Cursed be everyone who curses you, and blessed be those who bless you!**" (Genesis 27:26-29).

This reflects the power of the father's blessing upon his children. In Scripture you can clearly see a pattern of how the covenant blessing of God transfers from the father to his children. In a later chapter I will reveal how the enemy steals the Believer's wealth inheritance through the destruction of the family unit.

In Genesis 35:9-14, God confirms the blessing that Isaac had conferred upon his son Jacob. Not only does God release the covenant blessing upon Jacob, but He also changes his name from Jacob to Israel. I mentioned earlier that when you come into agreement with God's plan for your life, you receive a new name. Jacob started out crooked and deceitful, but there was a word spoken over his life that could not be annulled. God was committed to Jacob because of the covenant He had in place with Abraham and Isaac. I'm going somewhere with this thought, so keep reading.

Then God appeared to Jacob again, when he came from Padan Aram, and blessed him. And God said to him, "Your name is Jacob; your name shall not be called Jacob anymore, but Israel shall be your name." **So He called his name Israel. Also God said to him: "I am God Almighty. Be fruitful and multiply; a nation and a company of nations shall proceed from you, and kings shall come from your body. The land which I gave Abraham and Isaac I give to you; and to your descendants after you I give this land." Then God went up from him in the place where He talked with him.** So Jacob set up a pillar in the place where He talked with him, a pillar of stone; and he poured a drink offering on it, and he poured oil on it. (Genesis 35:9-14 KJV)

You have not been left out of this great wealth transfer, my beloved. I declare that your time has come to come out of the land of just enough, not enough, and nothing at all. I hope your faith has been stirred to kick the devil out and possess your wealth inheritance.

But the Scripture has confined all under sin that the promise by faith in Jesus Christ might be given to those who believe, (Galatians 3:22 KJV).

I have one question. Do you BELIEVE in Jesus? If your answer is yes then by faith you can receive the promise of the covenant. The promise can only be released to those who believe. The sad thing is that there are many Christians who believe in Jesus but they don't believe they can or should live a prosperous life. The promises of God can only manifest where there is faith. If you do not believe then you will not receive.

The church I grew up in taught me that poverty was a sign of humility and to settle for what was a broke, busted and disgusting life. Who wants to struggle and live in lack all their life? Not I and I hope not you! Those teachings resulted in me perceiving God as someone who was harsh, distant and cold. For a long time, I really believed that God dealt me a bad hand in life and that He created me to struggle. Have you ever heard the saying that everybody wasn't created to be rich? Well, I bought into that lie and believed that there was no need to seek more. I thought I was in the class of those chosen to be poor. Do you know how many Christians believe this same lie or something similar to it? I later learned that the devil wanted me to believe this way in order to keep me from effectively executing the purpose and plan of God for my life.

I believe the biggest and most destructive lie, in the heart of the Church, is that Jesus was poor. I believe a lot of people equate the humility, suffering and sacrifice that was exemplified by Christ as poverty. Unconsciously, I believed it was wrong to ask for my needs to be met when Jesus had sacrificed so much for me already. Once the Holy Spirit revealed the truth to me, I made a firm commitment to destroy the lies of the enemy. My goal is to reach and teach as many people as possible the truth about their wealth inheritance, and help them to recover all.

Before we move on I want you to search your heart for a moment. What are some of your fears and unconscious beliefs about asking God to meet your needs? Have you subconsciously bought into the lie that Jesus was poor or that it is wrong to ask God to bless you? The devil is a liar! I will show you in Scripture that Jesus was not poor when He was on earth—He became poor so you could become rich.

For we know the grace of our Lord, though He was rich yet for your sakes He became poor that through His poverty you might become rich. (2 Cor. 8:9)

Chapter Seven

THE WEALTH ESTATE OF CHRIST

Every Scripture is God-breathed (given by His inspiration) and profitable for instruction, for reproof and conviction of sin, for correction of error and discipline in obedience, [and] for training in righteousness (in holy living, in conformity to God's will in thought, purpose, and action), so that the man of God may be complete and proficient, well fitted and thoroughly equipped for every good work. (2 Timothy 3:16,17AMP).

A major paradigm shift *(correction of error)* is needed in the Body of Christ, especially in the area of money. The church teaches on many subjects; however, when it comes to money there seems to be a big *"Do Not Enter,"* sign posted. It seems that from the pulpit to the pew there is a silent agreement in place that money is evil; therefore, it should not be discussed. I often wonder if those who hold so tightly to this code of silence even recognize that the management of money is the second most discussed subject in the Bible. Research has revealed that there are at least 2,350 verses in the Bible that discuss money. It seems to me that money was an important matter in the heart of God. He *inspired* the over 2,000

Scriptures written about money. I am confounded by the number of born-again brothers and sisters who recognize the Bible as God's Word, yet they refuse to have faith in what He has promised. If Scripture is God breathed and given by His inspiration *(and it is)*, then you have to make a decision to trust God's Word and believe that what He has said can and will come to pass. God's promises, prophecies, and principles as set forth in His Word cannot fail when received by faith.

Seek out of the book of the Lord and read: not one of these [details of prophecy] shall fail, none shall want and lack her mate [in fulfillment]. For the mouth [of the Lord] has commanded, and His Spirit has gathered them. (Isaiah 34:16 AMP)

Upon close examination of my own life, I found I had a lot of unchallenged assumptions keeping me in bondage financially. Assumptions are things you believe to be true without studying the facts for yourself. These assumptions are usually strongly held beliefs that have been established by the opinion of credible people. I stated earlier how in my formative years, some of the churches I attended influenced the thought that poverty was the will of God. I in turn *assumed* this to be true since there seemed to be a consensus amongst other credible authorities in my life. Phrases such as, "You need to be content with what you have—there are people worse off than you," seemed to be true since they were to some degree backed by Scripture. However, I later recognized, contentment means to be grateful for what you have—it does not mean you have to settle for where you are.

The most erroneous and damaging teaching that I received was that *Jesus was poor.* My father and husband both served 20 years in the United States Army, which afforded me the unique opportunity to travel around the world and experience various cultures first hand. In my travels I discovered a common assumption held by many Foreign and American Christians alike—on the average they unconsciously assume Jesus was poor. I also noticed the same code of silence existed in relation to discussing money in the Church—*"Do Not Enter!"*

I must inform you that contrary to popular belief and the unchallenged assumptions held by so many, *Jesus Was Not Poor!* Now hold onto your seat and keep reading! Okay, have you calmed down? I know that was probably a shock to your belief system, nevertheless, it is true. I believe this chapter is worth the cost of the entire book. See my friend, as long as you subconsciously believe that Jesus was poor you will always feel guilty about desiring to have a prosperous life. Guilt will automatically cause you to shut down your God given desire to multiply. It will convince you to settle for a life of mediocrity. God's will is for you to prosper and live an abundant life.

Are you ready to challenge your unchallenged assumptions concerning the financial status of Jesus while He walked the earth? If so, then follow me on this journey through Scripture and allow the Holy Spirit to reveal to you that *Jesus Was Not Poor."*

Jesus transferred His wealth to you at Calvary!

For you know the grace of our Lord Jesus Christ, **that though He was rich,** yet for your sakes **He became poor, that you through His poverty might become rich,** (2 Corinthians 8:9 NKJV).

Please Stop! Do not proceed any further! Sit still until your spirit catches the revelation contained in the above Scripture. Every time I read this verse I get excited! Jesus was very rich, but He gave it all up so that you and I could become rich through Him. Wow! God saw that man was moving farther and farther away from the purpose and plan for which He had created him, so he sent Jesus to redeem His creation. Remember, Genesis 1:26-28 states:

Then God said, "Let Us make man in Our image, according to Our likeness; let them have dominion…over all the earth and over every creeping thing that creeps on the earth." So God created man in His own image; in the image of God He created him; male and female He created them. Then God blessed them, and God said to them, "Be fruitful and multiply; fill the earth and subdue it; have dominion…over every living thing that moves on the earth."

God's purpose for man, as revealed in Scripture is very clear and cannot be refuted. He created man to be fruitful, to multiply, and to have dominion over the earth. In the Garden of Eden there was no such thing as poverty and lack. Adam and Eve were abundantly furnished and equipped to fulfill the assignment God had given to them. Poverty was not in the plan! Poverty was introduced when Adam and Eve heard and obeyed a voice other than God's. In the same way poverty, lack, and insufficiency only exist where the voice of God is not heard and obeyed. Jesus, on the other hand, came to restore to God and man that which was lost in the Garden:

...And that He may send Jesus Christ, who was preached to you before, **whom heaven must receive until the times of restoration of all things**, which God has spoken by the mouth of all His holy prophets since the world began, (Acts 3:20,21KJV).

Jesus serves as the mediator to bring God and man back into a right relationship so God's purpose can be fulfilled in heaven and on earth. Through the blood sacrifice of Jesus, not only have we been saved from eternal destruction, but we have also been restored to power and authority as God's representatives in the earth realm. God did not send Jesus to the earth without the proper resources and provision to fulfill His assignment. Jesus walked in both natural and supernatural provision. This provision included a home, transportation, money, food, clothing, etc. You and I are no different. God knows you need provision in order to fulfill what He has commissioned you to do. Let us look to Jesus as our example and destroy the lies of the devil.

Through Jesus you can now live an Abundant Life that Overflows:

The thief comes only in order to steal and kill and destroy. **I came that they may have and enjoy life, and have it in abundance (to the full,**

till it overflows) (John 10:10 AMP).

In chapter six you saw how God's covenant promise was transferred from one generation to the next. This pattern is revealed in the earthly lineage of Jesus as well. Joseph was a descendent from the line of David and was also the earthly father of Jesus. The first thing I want you to see is that Jesus was born into the earthly family of a wealthy man as revealed in Luke 2:4.

Joseph also went up from Galilee, out of the city of Nazareth, into Judea, to the city of David, which is called Bethlehem, *because he was of the house and lineage of David...*

David was an extremely wealthy king. He financed the House of God that his son Solomon built out of his personal treasure. Listen as David speaks:

"Moreover, because of my delight in the house of my God, *I now give my personal treasures of gold and silver for the house of my God over and above all that I've provided for the holy house:* 100 tons of gold (gold of Ophir) and 250 tons of refined silver for overlaying the walls of the buildings, the gold for the gold [work] and the silver for the silver, for all the work to be done by the craftsmen. Now, who will volunteer to consecrate himself to the LORD today?" (1 Chronicles 29:3-5 AMP).

Can you imagine financing the "House of God" out of your own personal treasure? Well, that's exactly what David did. I don't have the exact math but I do know that what he gave was in the millions (plural). David was definitely a "Kingdom Expansion Million-Heir!" The main point is that Joseph who was from the house and lineage of David who was both wealthy and rich!

A lot of people subconsciously believe that Joseph was poor because Jesus was born in a manger. Wrong! Joseph was taxed because he was wealthy. They went to the stable because the Inn was overbooked:

And she brought forth her firstborn Son, and wrapped Him in swaddling clothes, and laid Him in a manger, *because there was no room for them in the inn* (Luke 2:4-7KJV).

Joseph owned and raised Jesus in a house:

When they saw the star, they rejoiced with exceedingly great joy. *And when they had come into the house,* they saw the young Child with Mary His mother, and fell down and worshiped Him, *(Matthew 2:10 KJV).*

The earthly life and ministry of Jesus was in part funded by King Herod during his infancy:

…And when they **had opened their treasures, they presented gifts to Him: gold, frankincense, and myrrh** (Matthew 2:11 KJV).

How many people do you know that bring Gold as a gift to new-born babies today? Hum! The King sent a treasure to Jesus that included gold (money). I pray that the eyes of your understanding are being opened to see that Jesus was provided with the best of the best.

Jesus owned his own home and entertained overnight guests:

Jesus turned around and saw them following. He said to them, *"What are you looking for?"* They answered, "Teacher, where are you staying?" *He said to them, "Come and see." They followed Him and saw where He lived.* They stayed with Him that day. It was about four o'clock in the afternoon (John 1:38-40 NLV).

There are certain statements made by Jesus himself that would lead one to believe that He was poor. Here is an example of a few such statements:

Now it happened as they journeyed on the road, *that* someone said to Him, "Lord, I will follow You wherever You go." *And Jesus said to him, "Foxes have holes and birds of the air have nests, but the Son of Man has nowhere to lay His head."* (Luke 9:57-58 KJV).

Jesus was not saying that He did not have anywhere to live! If you read the verses above this passage in the Bible you will find that the disciples had gone before Jesus to make preparations for His journey to Jerusalem. In other words, they were making hotel accommodations for Him in the towns He had to pass through. They entered a village of Samaria and the people refused to allow Jesus to stay there because they were enemies of the Jews (see John 4:9). In His response, Jesus is referring to the rejection He had received from the Samaritans and to the persons motives for wanting to follow Him. The person who wanted to follow Jesus saw something in the natural that he was attracted to. I believe the attraction was to the fame he perceived to be associated with following Jesus (prestige, wealth, large crowds, free travel etc.) without recognizing the cost associated with what he saw. The man saw the outward fame—Jesus knew the unseen sacrifice of His ministry. In short, Jesus was looking for people committed to advancing God's kingdom, not their personal agenda.

Jesus had a large traveling ministry with a paid ministry team (the disciples) along with faith partners who supported His ministry financially. In *Luke 9:1,* Jesus chooses the twelve disciples and sends them forth to minister in His name. In *Luke 10:1,* He commissions another advance team of seventy more disciples. As you read both passages you find that Jesus instructed them to leave their money and purses at home. Now if you only read those passages, it seems as though He's telling them to give up their wealth as a condition of joining His ministry. Not so my friend! I submit to you that Jesus is breaking their dependency on the world's system of provision. He is training them in the area of faith and trust in God's supernatural provision. After all Jesus is preparing to leave them and they will have to know how to conduct ministry and handle the danger associated with it in His absence. How do I know this?

Look at *Luke 22:35-36:*

And He said to them, "When I sent you without money bag, knapsack, and sandals, did you lack anything?*" **So they said, "Nothing."** Then He said to them, **"But now, he who has a money bag, let him take it,** and likewise a knapsack; and he who has no sword, let him sell his garment and buy one.

Friend, I hope it is sinking deep within your spirit that the word *"lack"* does not exist in the Kingdom of God. First of all, the disciples had to have money to begin with if Jesus had to instruct them to leave it. Secondly, they obviously received compensation on their journey since they replied to Jesus that they lacked nothing while they were gone. After passing this test of faith, Jesus instructed them to take their personal items with them to include a *money-bag!* Why would the disciples need to carry a moneybag if Jesus required them to give up their earthly wealth? I reiterate here that: *Jesus Was Not Poor and neither were His disciples.* Guess what? You should not settle for lack in your life either.

Jesus was prepared to buy lunch for more than five thousand people in Luke 9:13-14:

But He said to them, **"You give them something to eat."** And they said, "We have no more than five loaves and two fish, **unless we go and buy food for all these people."** For there were about five thousand men. Then He said to His disciples, "Make them sit down in groups of fifty."

Again, in John 4:8 we see the disciples going to buy meat:

(For his disciples were gone away unto the city to buy meat.)

There were wealthy women who supported the ministry of Jesus as noted in Luke 8:2:

...And certain women who had been healed of evil spirits and infirmities—Mary called Magdalene, out of whom had come seven demons, and Joanna the wife of Chuza, Herod's steward, and Susanna, *and many others who provided for Him from their substance.*

Jesus and the Disciples owned *"Ships"* by which they traveled.

I'm sure you will agree that there is a grave difference between a canoe, a boat, and a ship. I recently took a cruise on a huge ship that was very luxurious—it had more rooms than I could count. It helped me realize why the Disciples had such a hard time getting to Jesus during the storm. Jesus traveled by ship and there was a fleet of ships traveling with Him according to Mark 4:36:

And when they had sent away the multitude, they took him even as he was in the ship. And there were also with him other little ships.

In a very disheartening discussion between Jesus and a rich young ruler (Mark 10:17-22), it can be clearly seen that the primary thing Jesus was trying to do was to turn him from trust in his earthly wealth to placing his trust in God's provision. This is still the call of Christ today. Examine the story of the rich young ruler:

Now as He was going out on the road, one came running, knelt before Him, and asked Him, "Good Teacher, what shall I do that I may inherit eternal life?" So Jesus said to him, "Why do you call Me good? No one *is* good but One, *that is,* God. You know the commandments: 'Do not commit adultery,' 'Do not murder,' 'Do not steal,' 'Do not bear false witness,' 'Do not defraud,' 'Honor your father and your mother.'" And he answered and said to Him, "Teacher, all these things I have kept from my youth." *Then Jesus, looking at him, loved him, and said to him, "One thing you lack: Go your way,* **sell whatever you have and give to the poor, and you will have treasure in heaven;** and come, take up the cross, and follow Me." **But he was sad at this word, and went away sorrowful, for he had great possessions.** (Lk. 10:17-22)

Then Jesus looked around and said to His disciples, **"How hard it is for those who have riches to enter the kingdom of God!"** And the disciples were astonished at His words. But Jesus answered again and said to them, "Children, how hard it is **for those who trust in riches to enter the kingdom of God!** (Luke 10:23-24 KJV)

It is easier for a camel to go through the eye of a needle than for a rich man to enter the kingdom of God." **And they were greatly astonished, saying** *among themselves, "Who then can be saved?"* But Jesus looked at them and said, "With men *it is* impossible, but not with God; for with God all things are possible." *Then Peter began to say to Him, "See, we have left all and followed You."* (Luke 10:25-28 KJV)

Do you see that everyone in this passage is wealthy, not just the rich young ruler? Immediately, upon hearing the comment of Jesus the people raised objections. Why? They were all rich! In verse 28, Peter even became defensive—proving again that Jesus was wealthy. Based on Peter's response he had to be referring to their present status. He said, "Lo, we have left all and followed you *(someone who is rich),* and now You tell us we will not be able to go to heaven," (emphasis added).

Jesus answers Peter with a promise that still stands for you today:

So Jesus answered and said, *"Assuredly, I say to you, there is no one* who has left house or brothers or sisters or father or mother or wife or children or lands, for My sake and the gospel's, **who shall not receive a hundredfold now in this time—houses and brothers and sisters and mothers and children and lands, with persecutions—and in the age to come, eternal life,** (Luke 10:29-30 KJV).

Jesus has promised that those who will commit to advancing the kingdom of God will not only receive eternal life, but a hundredfold return in this life as well. Do you remember that Isaac received a hundred times more than what he sowed—in the same year? Now it is your turn to sow and reap.

The promise included material possessions *(houses, lands)* which makes it even clearer that God does not want you to be broke in this life. He wants you to own *lands with houses* upon it. I dare you to stand up and start claiming your real estate in Jesus Name!

Take a break and meditate on Mark 10:29-30. Jesus was not condemning wealth or the desire for wealth—He condemned placing your trust in wealth above God. God is ready to release the hundredfold blessing in your life right now and this book holds, the Spiritual Principles to Access Your Wealth Inheritance. I know by now you are saying, "Okay! Enough already, I have the revelation and I am ready to acquire *"Spirit Led Wealth,"* but we have just a few more *principles* to discover before you are able launch into your wealthy place. Look at 2 Corinthians 8:9 one more time before we move on:

For you know the grace of our Lord Jesus Christ, **that though He was rich**, yet for your sakes **He became poor, that you through His poverty might become rich.**

I really want you to allow this truth to sink into your heart. You have to erase the erroneous beliefs that you hold about Jesus and wealth. If you do not make this critical transition in your heart you will not be able to manifest the abundant life that Christ intended for you to live.

I want to provide you with everything I possibly can to help you break free from the negative influences that may be holding you captive so let us move into the financial deliverance portion of this teaching. In the next two chapters you will discover the schemes and deceptions used by the enemy to blind and block you from receiving your wealth inheritance. Then I will show you how to get it all back once and for all!

Chapter Eight

"DAMAGED HEART DRIVES"

...*"And be constantly renewed in the spirit of your mind [having a fresh mental and spiritual attitude],* (Ephesians 4:23 AMP)

The reason you are where you are right now is because of the way you think. Yeah, that's right! The way you think is the culprit that is keeping you captive to your present circumstances, *"As a man thinketh in his heart so is he."(Proverbs 23:7KJV)* Another passage of scripture encourages us to, *"Keep your heart with all diligence for out of it springs the issues of life."* _____(Proverbs 4:23)

Before you can create a lifestyle of wealth you must first uncover the thought patterns that caused you to create a life of mediocrity. The *spirit of your mind* mentioned in Ephesians 4:23, indicates that there is an invisible force controlling the way you think. This invisible force *(spirit)* is guiding and directing every decision you make in life. You are either guided by the "law of the spirit of life and peace in Christ Jesus," or the "law of sin and death" (Romans 8:2). It is impossible to be guided by both laws simultaneously. The flesh is always in opposition to the Spirit of God;

therefore, decisions made from this realm keep you in sin (opposition to God) and produce destruction and death.

The devil's desire is to keep you in a cycle of sin and death because he knows that dead things cannot produce, grow, or multiply. On the other hand, when you operate under the control of the Holy Spirit there are no limits to your ability to produce. In short, you cannot expect your life to change until you "Take the Limits Off" and transform your mind to God's way of doing things on purpose. This means you have to make a conscious effort to transform your mind—it will not happen automatically!

I say then, walk by the Spirit and you will not carry out the desire of the flesh. For the flesh desires what is against the Spirit, and the Spirit desires what is against the flesh; these are opposed to each other, so that you don't do what you want. (Galatians 5:16-17).

Learning something is one thing, but applying what you have learned is totally different. Have you ever heard the Scripture *"Faith without works is dead?"* it means that you have to put action with your faith. Acquired knowledge is only information until it is put into proper use. I do not want to be guilty of giving you a lot of information and not tell you how to properly apply it. I want you to receive Y*our Wealth Inheritance,* so together we can *Advance the Kingdom of God on Earth.*

In order for the truth of God's Word to take root in your heart, you have to examine your belief system and old patterns of thinking. In my personal life, although I tithed, sowed seeds of faith, and created budget after budget, I still found myself stagnant and unable to progress financially. I also saw many other faithful Christians experiencing the same difficulty.

In short I saw how the church was full of honest, God fearing people who looked prosperous outwardly but financially challenged. The reason I can talk about this is because I was guilty of this myself. I realized I did not need more money, a better job or prayer—I needed a change of heart and a whole new mindset!

Through much prayer and meditation the Lord revealed to me there was a major epidemic infecting and damaging my personal life and many others in the Body of Christ as well. He said to me, "Sonya, you— like so many of my children," have *"Damaged Heart Drives.* He then said, "Your, *heart* has been *infected and damaged* with erroneous information—causing your appetite to change and now this deception has *driven you away from My principles."* The Lord then confirmed what He said by leading me to *Amos 2:4* which says:

Thus says the LORD: "For three transgressions of Judah, and for four, I will not turn away its punishment, because they have despised the law of the LORD, and have not kept His commandments. ***Their lies lead them astray, lies which their fathers followed.***

Talk about a *"in your face"* Word! God had my full attention on this one and I was determined to search the matter out. Judah was being punished for refusing to follow God's way and not keeping His commandments. The scripture reveals that their lies had lead them astray and worst of all the lies were from their fathers. Huh? *Lies which their fathers followed?* I quickly began to understand what God meant by *"Damaged Heart Drives."*

God said, "The hearts of my people have been infected with lies—lies planted by the enemy, into the hearts of the fathers, which have been passing from generation to generation. These lies *infect the hearts* of my people, causing them to be *driven away* from following my commandments. This is why so many of my children are unable to possess and walk in the *wealth inheritance* I have left for them." After hearing this in my spirit, I remembered *Exodus 20:1-6:*

And God spoke all these words, saying: "I *am* the LORD your God, who brought you out of the land of Egypt, out of the house of bondage. "You shall have no other gods before Me. "You shall not make for yourself a carved image—any likeness *of anything* that *is* in heaven above, or that *is* in the earth beneath, or that *is* in the water under the earth; you shall not bow down to them nor serve them. *For I, the LORD your* God, am a jealous God, visiting the iniquity of the fathers upon the children to the third and fourth generations of those who hate Me, but showing mercy to thousands, to those who love Me and keep My commandments. (Exodus 20:1-6 KJV)

The passage in Exodus reveals that the *"Curses"* or *"Error"* of the father's, transfers from one generation to the next in the same way the c*ovenant promises,* are transferred. The enemy knows that the most influential person in your life is your father. With this in mind, it is easy to understand why the devil wants to destroy the family unit. Once the enemy plants his lies in the father's heart, the mindset is then established in the family and passed from one generation to the next. Are you seeing the light yet? For the purpose of this book the word *father* can be taken in the literal sense, or as representing the credible people who influenced and shaped your way of thinking (parents, teacher's, pastors, etc.).

Right now you might be saying, "Yeah, I hear you Sonya, but I am the righteousness of God and Jesus has removed the curse for me." You are absolutely right! According to Galatians 3:13, Jesus became a curse for you, but He did not abolish the existence of curses.

Curses are still operative today. A *curse* is defined as, *"the invoking of evil on a person; and affliction"* (p. 20, Webster, 2006). It further defines the word *afflict* as to: *"distress with mental or bodily pain; torment."* Sounds like part of satan's job description, and it is. Why? Because he is the one who still has the power to invoke or inflict curses. He is looking for any foothold he can find to invoke a curse or enforce one that is already established in your family line.

"Be sober, be vigilant; because your adversary the devil walks about like a roaring lion, seeking whom he may devour" (1 Peter 5:8 KJV).

According to Proverbs 26:2, *"...A curse without cause cannot come."* This reveals that the devil has to have an open door before he can invoke a curse upon you. What better does he have to do this than through a lie *(teaching contrary to God),* received from your fathers—*credible authorities who influenced your beliefs.* These lies and curses of the enemy take root in your soul and once they are established they become *"Emotional Roadblocks to Wealth."*

Jesus paid the penalty to set you free; but you are responsible for maintaining that freedom. *It Is Not Automatic!* Jesus removed the curse—you are responsible for keeping the door closed. Take another moment to pause and think on these things! Now, let us identify and destroy the *"Emotional Road Blocks,"* that may be responsible for keeping you from receiving *Your Wealth Inheritance.*

Chapter Nine

8 Emotional Road Blocks to Wealth

A good man out of the good treasure of his **heart** brings forth good; and an evil man out of the evil treasure of his **heart** brings forth evil. For out of the **abundance** of the **heart** his mouth speaks. (Luke 6:45).

Of all the "Spiritual Keys" throughout this book, this is one of the most important ones, *"You must become inwardly wealthy before you will ever produce external wealth."* The abundance of your heart determines the fruit that will be produced in your life. I want you to hear me in the spirit, "It is solely your responsibility to produce the type of life you want to live." From this day forward I want you to stop accusing, blaming or holding anyone else responsible for your future.

Have you ever wondered why so many people who win the lottery or inherit large sums of money end up broke? They gained external riches without the internal wealth to maintain it. In the same way, it will be impossible to unlock and maintain your *Wealth Inheritance,* without first removing the *Emotional*

Roadblocks to Wealth, and submitting to God's way of doing things.

Emotional Roadblocks are the invisible forces *(spirits)* guiding your decisions as I mentioned earlier. In my personal life I found eight *Emotional Roadblocks* that were hindering my ability to become financially free. There may be more, but I guarantee that when you get free in these eight areas you will begin to immediately feel inwardly wealthy and you will gain the strength to begin producing external wealth as well.

The Emotional Road Blocks to Wealth:

1. The Roadblock of Pride: Blocks You from asking God and others for help. Pride is the refusal to acknowledge the truth about your financial condition in order to maintain status, credibility, or admiration from others. Self-exaltation, self-preservation, and self-protection are all forms of pride that keep a person dependent on themselves rather than God. Just about every family I know has pride in their family name. Statements such as: "You are a Johnson, and Johnson's lead the way," "What happens in the Johnson house stays in the Johnson house," or "You better not ask nobody for nothing—you are a Johnson."

When you hear statements like this, over and over, it builds a lie in your mind to cause you to believe you cannot show any weakness or ask anybody for help. Pride keeps you operating in pretense! Nobody has it all together. We all need help! God told us to ASK for what we need!

Pride goes before **destruction,** and a **haughty spirit** before a fall." (Proverbs 16:18 NKJV)

"Therefore **humble yourselves** under the mighty hand of God, that **He may exalt you in due time, casting all your care upon Him, for He cares for you."** (1 Peter 5:6-7 NJKV)

"Ask, and it will be given to you; seek, and you will find; knock, and it will be opened to you. For everyone who asks receives, and he who seeks finds, and to him who knocks it will be opened." (Matthew 7:7-8 NKJV)

The opposite of pride is humility before God. Pride is the root of all destruction. Turn to God and He will exalt you in every area in which you are experiencing lack.

2. The Road Block of the Threefold Cord of Shame, Guilt and Condemnation: Blocks You from Entering the Presence of God: This threefold-cord is put in place when a person perceives he has violated a boundary that in turn produces regret *(guilt)* and a strong feeling of unworthiness *(shame)* within the individual. The person then passes judgment on themselves *(condemns),* as useless or incapable of acceptance. The enemy plants the lie that you are worthless and undeserving of prosperity. You feel guilty about the financial choices you have made; as a result, you are ashamed of your financial state—condemning yourself as undeserving of or incapable of producing wealth.

This threefold cord is also the major enemy of worship and prayer. A person, who believes the lie that they are unworthy and unacceptable, will not readily enter the presence of God in worship. The enemy does not want you to pray or worship because he knows that in the presence of God there is fullness of joy. Worship is based on God's worth not our own!

For the Scripture says, **"Whoever believes on Him will not be put to shame."** For there is no distinction between Jew and Greek, **for the same Lord over all is rich to all who call upon Him.** For **"whoever calls on the name of the LORD shall be saved."** (Romans 10:11-13 NKJV)

We have all sinned and fallen short of the glory of God (Romans 3:23 NKJV), making us all guilty as charged. However, once you accepted Jesus as your personal Savior, He erased the charges and now you are free from the guilt, shame and condemnation of your past actions. Rejoice in the truth that: *"You can come boldly to the throne of grace and find help in the time of need"* (Hebrews 4:16 NKJV) and *"You can do* **all things through Christ who strengthens you."** (Philippians 4:13 NKJV)

"There is, therefore, now no condemnation to those who are in Christ Jesus, who do not walk according to the flesh, but according to the Spirit" (Romans 8:1 NKJV).

3. The Road Block of Un-forgiveness: Blocks You from Forgiving or Receiving Forgiveness. This is the one spirit that completely shuts the windows of heaven up in your life. To forgive is to release someone who has caused you injury or harm. It is accomplished when you relinquish your desire to get revenge or punish the other person. You no longer hold them guilty as charged. Forgiveness is what keeps you free to receive from God, especially during times when you need to be forgiven. *"Forgiving others does not make them right—it just makes you free!"*

"But if you do not forgive, neither will your Father forgive your trespasses." (Mark 11:26)

"If we confess our sins, He is faithful and just to forgive us our sins and to cleanse us from all unrighteousness." (1John 1:9 NKJV)

"Beloved, do not avenge yourselves, but rather give place to wrath; for it is written, **"Vengeance is Mine, I will repay," says the Lord.** Therefore "If your enemy is hungry, feed him; if he is thirsty, give him a drink; for in so doing you will heap coals of fire on his head." Do not be overcome by evil, but overcome evil with good" (Romans 12:19-21 NKJV).

When you make the choice to forgive, God promises to recompense you for the damage caused by those that harm you. God is going to make it up to you, so let them go!

4. The Road Block of Anger: Blocks the Flow of Giving and Receiving in Relationships: Anger is a strong emotion of resentment held against someone or something. God has created you for relationship with Himself and others. When a spirit of anger fills your heart, it blocks you from being able to properly give and receive in those relationships. God releases His blessings to you through people! The person you become angry with just may be the person holding your blessing. I found in my financial relationship with money that I was often angry that there wasn't enough money—in reality the reason I didn't have enough money was because I was angry.

"By this all will know that you are My disciples, if you have love for one another" (John 13:35 NKJV)

"Be angry, and do not sin:" do not let the sun go down on your wrath, nor give place to the devil." (Ephesians 4:26-27 NKJV).

"Give, and it shall be given unto you; good measure, pressed down, and shaken together, and running over, **shall men give into your bosom. For with the same measure that ye mete withal it shall be**

measured to you again."(Luke 6:38)

5. The Road Block of Fear (Doubt/Unbelief): Blocks Your Ability to Trust God: The average person would say that they have no fear. I beg to differ. Fear is the most deeply rooted of all the negative emotions. Fear is a perceived risk that prevents a person from taking action. Faith is the opposite of fear and requires you to believe without evidence. *"Now faith is the substance of things hoped for, the evidence of things not seen"* (Hebrews 11:1 KJV). It takes faith to trust, pray, tithe and give to a person you cannot physically see—God. The enemy plays the fear card by planting the lie that God will not fulfill His promises, *for you.* There are several types of fear—fear of the unknown, fear of failing, fear of responsibility, fear of losing, fear of success, fear of tithing etc. Fear causes you to be stingy and hold tightly to what you have. Doubt and unbelief are also forms of fear. A person who is in doubt will never have any assurance (confidence) in God's Word. Doubt interrupts the process of faith and prevents you from inheriting the promises of God.

Faith is what pleases God, *"But without faith it is impossible to please Him, for he who comes to* God must believe that He is, and that **He is a rewarder** of those who diligently seek Him." (Hebrews 11:6 NKJV)

"...Because fear involves torment. But he who fears has not been made perfect in love." (1 John 4:18 NKJV)

So Jesus answered and said to them, "Have faith in God. For assuredly, I say to you, **whoever says** to this mountain, 'Be removed and be cast into the sea,' **and does not doubt in his heart, but believes that those things he says will be done, he will have whatever he says. Therefore I say to you, whatever things you ask when you pray, believe that you receive them, and you will have them.**" (Mark 11:22-24 NKJV)

"**But let him ask in faith, with no doubting,** for he who doubts is like a wave of the sea driven and tossed by the wind. **For let not that man suppose that he will receive anything from the Lord; he is a double-minded man, unstable in all his ways.**" (James 1:6-8 NKJV)

"**For God has not given us a spirit of fear**, but of power and of love and of a sound mind," (2 Tim. 1:7 NKJV).

God says, "Fear not, for I *am* with you, be not dismayed, for I *am* your God. I will strengthen you, *Yes, I will help you, I will uphold you with My righteous right hand'* (Isaiah 41:10 NKJV). God can be trusted to take care of you!

6. **The Road Block of Comparison/Impatience: Blocks Your Ability to be grateful as you wait on the Lord:** This particular roadblock is

the cause of so much debt accumulation. Comparison opens the door to a whole army of negative influences such as: jealousy, envy, intimidation, inferiority, inadequacy, fear, depression etc. A book could be written on this one by itself. The comparison trap keeps you from being grateful to God for what you have. It causes you to compare and measure yourself by a standard (usually other people) established outside of God. Comparison leads to impatience which causes you to operate in the buy now pay later cycle in order to keep up appearances. Comparison also causes you to never be able to be satisfied—you become so busy looking at everybody else's roses that you can't recognize or smell your own. The Bible is very clear that comparison is unwise. Read the following Scriptures.

For we dare not class ourselves or compare ourselves with those who commend themselves. But they, measuring themselves by themselves, and **comparing** themselves among themselves, are not wise. (2 Corinthians 10:12 NKJV)

My brethren, count it all joy when you fall into various trials, knowing that the testing of your faith produces patience. *But let patience have its perfect work, that you may be perfect and complete, lacking nothing.* (James 1:2-4 NKJV)

And we desire that each one of you show the same diligence to the full assurance of hope until the end, that you do not become sluggish, *but imitate those who through faith and patience inherit the promises.* (Hebrews 6:11-12 NKJV)

Commit your way to the LORD, trust also in Him, and He shall bring it to pass. He shall bring forth your righteousness as the light, and your justice as the noonday. Rest in the LORD, and *wait patiently* for Him; do not fret because of him who prospers in his way, because of the man who brings wicked schemes to pass. Cease from anger, and forsake wrath; do not fret—it only causes harm. For evildoers shall be cut off; *but those who wait on the LORD, they shall inherit the earth.* (Psalm 37:5-9)

7. The Road Block of Laziness: Blocks You From Taking Action. Some of the root lies of the spirit of laziness are: "Why bother—nobody cares," "you can't make a difference," "you don't have what it takes to do that," and "you'll never get out of debt so you might as well have fun." A person plagued by laziness allows life to happen rather than making life happen. Laziness causes a person to settle in mediocrity and lack because they refuse to take responsibility and act. The scriptures speak well about the end results of laziness:

"The soul of a lazy man desires, and has nothing; but the soul of the diligent shall be made rich" (Proverbs 13:4 NKJV).

"The lazy man will not plow because of winter; He will beg during harvest and have nothing."

"The desire of the lazy man kills him, for his hands refuse to labor" (Proverbs 21:25 NKJV).

"The hand of the diligent will rule, but the lazy man will be put to forced labor." (Prov. 12:24 NKJV)

"Seest thou a man diligent in his business? He shall stand before kings; he shall not stand before mean men." (Proverbs 22:29 KJV)

8. The Road Block of Bondage: Blocks You From Walking in Freedom and Enjoying Your *"Wealth Inheritance."* The spirit of bondage holds a person captive against their will. The end result of all of the aforementioned *"Emotional Roadblocks,"* is *"Bondage."* Although you have been set free by the *Blood of Jesus,* the devil wants to keep you bound emotionally and financially. The responsibility of Jesus was to set you free—it is your responsibility to stay free:

"...For by whom a person is overcome, by him also he is brought into bondage. For if, after they have escaped the pollutions of the world through the knowledge of the Lord and Savior Jesus Christ, **they are again entangled in them and overcome, the latter end is worse for them than the beginning"** (2Peter 2:19-20).

"Inasmuch then as the children have partaken of flesh and blood, He Himself likewise shared in the same, **that through death He might destroy him who had the power of death, that is, the devil, and release those who through fear of death were all their lifetime subject to bondage.** For indeed He does not give aid to angels, **but He does give aid to the seed of Abraham"** (Hebrews 2:14-16 NKJV).

"For you did not receive the spirit of bondage again to fear, but you received the Spirit of adoption by whom we cry out, "Abba, Father," (Romans 8:15 NKJV).

Lies! Lies! Lies! Who can deliver from all these lies? I am sure you might be thinking something close to that right now. I have good news. You are not stuck! The key to getting free is to first recognize that you have been bound. The devil is so sorry that you are reading this book right now because his lies are forever exposed. Jesus says to you: "My sheep hear my voice, and I know them, and they follow Me. And I give them eternal life, and they shall never perish; **neither shall anyone snatch them out of my hand. My Father,** who has given them to me, **is greater than all; and no one is able to snatch them out of My Father's hand. I and My Father are one."** (John 10:27-30 NKJV). That's right! Nobody, not even the devil with his lies, can snatch you out of Jesus hands. However, the enemy can prevent you from living the abundant and prosperous life that Jesus promised—if the "Emotional Roadblocks," remain in your life. Now, I love you too much to let that happen!

In Matthew 12:29, Jesus asks a question, *"Or else how can one enter into a strong man's house, and spoil his goods, except he first bind the strong man? And then he will spoil his house."* I believe it is time to bind what has been binding you! I mentioned in an earlier chapter that God has given you the power to bind and loose according to Matthew 18:19, and it reads, *"Assuredly, I say to you, whatever you bind on earth will be bound in heaven, and whatever you loose on earth will be loosed in heaven.* This means that whatever God has declared *unlawful*, you can declare unlawful and bind it from your life. Likewise, whatever God has declared *lawful*, you can declare lawful and loose it in your life. The key here is asking in agreement with what God has already established in His Word as lawful and unlawful. **(1John 5:14-15 NKJV)**

"Now this is the confidence that we have in Him, that if we ask anything according to His will, He hears us. And if we know that He hears us, whatever we ask, we know that we have the petitions that we have asked of Him,"

The "Emotional Road Blocks to Wealth," are not lawful in the Kingdom of God. Therefore, you must take authority and declare them unlawful in your life. Once the Road Blocks are removed you will then be able to access your *wealth inheritance*.

It is altar call time! Time to rid yourself of the *"Emotional Road Blocks to Your Wealth,"* I have already commanded your release through prayer in the spirit. The only thing you have to do is pray the following prayer aloud by faith. Jesus declares, *"Until now you have asked nothing in My Name. Ask, and you will receive, that your joy may be full"* (John 16:24 KJV). Pray this prayer:

Father, I come to you in the name of Jesus to ask your forgiveness for my sins and the sins of my fathers. Forgive us Lord for trusting in ourselves and the world's system and not in Your Word. Forgive us for turning our backs to you and shutting our ears from hearing Your Word.

Father, I forgive my fathers and every credible person for any lies or negative influences they transferred into my life. I no longer hold them responsible.

I ask You to forgive me for any lie or negative influence that I have transferred to those under my watch (family, friends, co-workers, neighbors etc.). I confess that I have sinned out of ignorance of your Word and I repent now in Jesus Name. Father I receive Your forgiveness and I thank You for cleansing me from all unrighteousness in Jesus name.

Father, as I stand before the courtroom of heaven, I humbly ask that you vindicate me and deliver me from the bondage of the enemy. I come boldly before your throne to ask for Your help. I stand in the authority of Jesus Christ to dethrone the "Emotional Road Blocks," that damaged my heart drive.

In the name of Jesus, my Lord, I break and free myself from all demonic influences; ungodly soul-ties to my family bloodline on both sides ten generations back. I break and release myself from every spirit of error and lie of the devil transferred to me from the credible people who influenced my life.

In Jesus name, I renounce satan and all demonic influences from my mind, thoughts and emotions completely. Father, in Jesus name I ask that you release Your warring angels to come and break in pieces every gate and cut asunder the bars of iron and every chain, fetter or bond that has been erected in my life by the enemy. I denounce every curse of failure mechanism sent to hinder my family from succeeding as heirs of God and joint-heirs with Christ. In Jesus name, I renounce and destroy the Emotional Road Blocks that have held me in bondage.

In the name of Jesus I bind up the spirit of:

Pride and I release humility in my life. I humble myself under the mighty hand of God and I trust Him to exalt me in due time. I am above only and not beneath in Christ!

In the name of Jesus, I bind up the spirit of:

Guilt, shame, and condemnation and I receive my freedom in Christ. I come boldly to the throne of grace by the blood of Jesus. I am redeemed from the hand of the enemy. There is no shame to them that trust in God. I choose to trust God!

In the name of Jesus, I renounce the spirit of:

Unforgiveness and I choose to forgive. I forgive everyone who has hurt me in any way. The Lord is my refuge and my strong tower; vengeance is His and He will repay me. The love of God is alive in my heart!

In the name of Jesus, I renounce the spirit of:

Anger/Torment and I receive peace and joy. I declare that my relationships are fruitful and blessed. Freely I give and freely I receive. God will keep me in perfect peace because my mind is stayed on Him.

In the name of Jesus, I renounce the spirit of:

Fear, doubt and unbelief and I place faith in the God of my salvation. I will trust in the Lord, for greater is He that is within me than he that is in the world. I declare now that I possess power, love and a sound mind. The victory that overcomes the world is my faith! I am an overcomer in Jesus Name!

In the name of Jesus, I renounce the spirit of:

Comparison and Impatience and I release confidence and trust and activate faith for the promises of God to flow in my life now. I shall have what I say in Jesus name. I walk in the fruit of patience!

In the name of Jesus, I renounce the spirit of:

Laziness and I operate in diligence, faithfulness and strength to take action. I declare that I am diligent in my Kingdom assignment and my gifts make room for me.

In the name of Jesus, I renounce the spirit of Spirit

Of Bondage and I walk in the liberty and freedom delivered through Christ. Jesus Christ has redeemed me from the curse; therefore, I command every one of these demon spirits to go in Jesus name. I am Free!

Now, satan the Lord God rebukes you in Jesus name! I command you to go where the spirit of God directs you. I render every one of your weapons powerless, inoperative and ineffective in my life and the life of my family members. In the name of Jesus, I destroy every spirit of retaliation from you that will attempt to come against me and those connected to me. I declare my freedom in Christ! I am free to reign in this life through Christ Jesus! I declare the love, joy and peace of God reign in my life, in Jesus name, I pray. Amen!

As He spoke these words, many believed in Him. Then Jesus said to those Jews who believed Him, "If you abide in My word, you are My disciples indeed. And you shall know the truth, and the truth shall make you free." (John 8:30-32 NKJV)

The Truth Shall Make You Free!

Chapter Ten

HEART DRIVE RESET

Congratulations! You are free from the bondage and lies of the enemy that were blocking your wealth inheritance in the spirit realm. Now, I want to give you the keys for manifesting and maintaining your freedom in the natural realm. After that, I will give you the Principles to *Access Your Wealth Inheritance.*

God created you as a tripartite being. This means that there are three parts to your existence—body, soul and spirit. The soul is where your mind, will, intellect, imagination and emotions are housed. The mind is your place of reasoning and it has three compartments within it. They are the conscious, subconscious and the conscience. The conscious compartment makes you aware of your surroundings, the subconscious processes information you receive and your conscience is the (*"heart drive"*) where your core beliefs are stored.

The subconscious mind guides your decisions, behavior and reactions based on the beliefs stored in your conscience. The subconscious mind will automatically reject information that contradicts your conscience beliefs. I hope you got all of that! In other words, you will have to renew your mind before you can effectively create a new life of abundance.

There are two important steps to the deliverance process. The first step is to bind the demonic strongholds and place your spiritual freedom in the realm of the spirit. You have accomplished the first step through the prayer you prayed in the previous chapter. The second step is to change your old way of thinking. This is done by *renewing* your mind with the truth of God's word. The prayer of release you just prayed set you free in the spirit realm; however, in the natural realm your subconscious mind is still set to your old way of thinking. Failure to renew (retrain) your mind will cause that old mindset to resurrect from the dead and takeover again. This is why so many people lose their deliverance. They fail to renew their old way of thinking with the Word of God.

Therefore, leaving the discussion of the elementary principles of Christ, let us go on to perfection, ***not laying again the foundation of repentance from dead works and of faith toward God,*** (Hebrews 6:1 KJV).

In order to change your conscience mind (stored beliefs), you must feed your subconscious mind with new information—until it records the information as truth to you. This is done through a process called meditation and confession. Meditation is the key that unlocks your destiny in the Spirit realm and confession is what establishes it in the earth realm. The Lord said to Joshua:

"This Book of the Law shall not depart from your mouth, but you shall meditate in it day and night, that you may observe to do according to all that is written in it. **For then you will make your way prosperous, and then you will have good success.** (Joshua 1:8 KJV).

God was preparing Joshua to continue the ministry of Moses. In order for Joshua to effectively execute his new assignment, he had to change his mindset from that of a follower to that of a leader. The instruction to Joshua was to meditate on God's word day and night. The definition of meditate is: to reflect on; ponder; plan or intend in the mind. Joshua was to meditate on the Word of God then plan his course of action to carry it out. This is the same course of action you must take in order to change your old way of thinking.

The promises and will of God are located in His Word—as you meditate upon them your mind will become renewed to God's plan for your life. However, in order to prosper and have good success you must act in obedience to the revelation of God's Word by faith.

Once you renew your mind through meditation; it is imperative that you confess the Word of God daily. Confession is simply saying what God has said in His Word. One of the primary purposes of confession is to strengthen your belief in God, His Word and His ability to help you.

But what saith it? **"The Word is nigh thee, even in thy mouth** and in thy heart," that is, the word of faith which we preach: **that if thou shalt confess with thy mouth** the Lord Jesus, and shalt believe in thine heart that God hath raised Him from the dead, thou shalt be saved. For with the heart man believeth unto righteousness, and with the mouth confession is made unto salvation, (Romans 10:8-10 NKJV).

In short, meditation is the Word of God in your heart while confession is the Word of God in your mouth—when you put the two together they produce a changed "mindset!" A new mind is what it takes to produce a new harvest in your life. Remember: "It is not going to happen automatically!"

I want to encourage you to meditate in the Word of God and confess the Word by faith every day. I am so excited about your deliverance and the financial freedom that is being produced in your life right now. Everything you have received up to this point was to prepare you for the revelation contained in the next chapter. I want you to stop and just worship the Father for a moment. Thank Him for guiding you to this book and giving you the "Spiritual Principles to Access Your Wealth Inheritance."

PROCEED WITH EXTREME CAUTION!

Chapter Eleven

THE WEALTHY PLACE

It has been revealed to you through Scripture that one of the avenues the enemy has used to plant lies in our hearts was through lies transferred from our fathers. You also learned that God visits the iniquity of the fathers upon the children to the third and fourth generations. Read Exodus 20:1-6 below:

For I, the LORD your God, am a jealous God, visiting the iniquity of the fathers upon the children to the third and fourth generations of those who hate Me, but showing mercy to thousands, to those who love Me and keep My commandments.

Four generations equals 160 years. Therefore, if you are younger than 160 years old there is a very strong chance that you are living under curses put in place by your forefathers. Pause a moment and think about your family heritage. Do you see poverty, lack, struggle, depression, addiction, sickness? If so, you are the key to breaking these curses and releasing the *'wealth inheritance'* for you and the future generations of your family line. Are you ready to be the Joshua or the Esther of your family? If so, pay close attention because the Holy Spirit is ready to impart a revelation that will set in motion the breakthrough to receiving your *wealth inheritance.*

Look at what Proverbs 13:22 says:

"A good man leaves an inheritance to his children's children, **but the wealth of the sinner** is *stored up* for the righteous."

As I was writing this chapter the Holy Spirit kept prompting me to pay closer attention to the above Scripture. As I meditated, I kept locking in on, *"The wealth of the sinner is laid up."* Then the Lord began to reveal how His blessings are transferred from one generation to the next through the hands of a *good* (righteous) man; curses on the other hand are transferred through the hands of a sinful man." He then showed me that curses do not have the power to make His promises void. God's Word, which is eternal, establishes His promises as eternal! The word of God cannot fail! A person invokes a curse upon himself through sin (disobedience) to the Word, thereby preventing God's promises from being activated. His promises cannot be released into the atmosphere in which a curse exists. As I read the verse again, I leaped for joy at what I saw. The best way for me to explain it to you is to have you read the verse again according to the revelation I received.

Read aloud, "A good (righteous) man (father) leaves an **inheritance** to his children's children, **but the wealth (inheritance) of the sinner (father) is stored up** (on reserve) for the righteous (children) to claim and receive. (emphasis added)."

But showing mercy to thousands, to those who love Me and keep My commandments (Exodus 20:6 KJV).

Beloved, do you see what I see? The context of the scripture is about what happens to the wealth of a good man versus the wealth of a sinner man. The wealth (inheritance) of a good man (father) passes to his children's children. The wealth of the sinful man (father) is stored up (on reserve) until a righteous *(child)* rises up to claim it! I believe that just might be you. Okay, you need to stop! Read that again! Now, shout halleluiah!

Let me clarify the difference between a good man and a sinful man. A good man (righteous) is a man who is obedient to the commandments of God. Abraham is an example of a good man. He raised his family in the fear and admonition of the Lord. On the other hand a sinful man is any man who is not submitted to the Lordship of Christ. Mind you, a sinful man can appear to be outwardly good—he is not necessarily a bad person. However, what makes him sinful is the fact that his heart is not submitted to the Lordship of Christ. The sinful man follows his own heart apart from God—his lack of obedience to God causes him and his family to be cursed. Eli and Saul are examples of men who followed their own heart rather than obeying the commandment of God. Outwardly both men seemed Godly—they were actually chosen by God; but their *heart drive was damaged*—causing them to lose God's promise. (See 1 Samuel 3:11-14 and 13:1-13). Thank God there is hope!

Despite the condition of your father's heart toward God, you are now the righteousness of God in Christ Jesus—you can come boldly to the throne of grace and claim your wealth inheritance. The promises of God that were forfeited through the disobedience of your fathers are still on reserve—waiting for you (the righteous) to rise up and claim them! God shows mercy to those who love Him and keep His commandments to a thousand generations. The only thing God is waiting for is someone in your family to commit to Him and His way—He shows mercy to those who love Him and keep His commandments. Are you the one? I believe so if you have made it this far.

I proudly announce that you have just become the *"Master Key"* to unlocking the *"Wealth Inheritance,"* for the next one thousand *generations* in your family line. Shout halleluiah!

Stand up and begin to call forth the *"wealth inheritance,"* stored up for you in Jesus Name! The ministries, ideas, businesses, wealth, and health that your fathers did not receive are now available to you! You are hereby authorized to call forth those things that be not (in your life) as though they were (to be), by the power invested in you as an *heir* of God and *joint-heir* with Christ.

Are you ready to receive *"Spirit-Led Wealth,"* and help me to reach as many people as possible with this liberating message, so they can receive the, *"Spiritual Principles to Access their Wealth Inheritance.*

I call heaven and earth as witnesses today against you, that I have set before you life and death, blessing and cursing; therefore choose life, that both you and your descendants may live; that you may love the LORD your God, that you may obey His voice, and that you may cling to Him, for He is your life and the length of your days; and that you may dwell in the land which the LORD swore to your fathers, to Abraham, Isaac, and Jacob, to give them."(Deuteronomy 30:19-20)

The beautiful thing about our heavenly Father is, He gives us all a choice. In the same way you made the choice to accept Jesus as your Lord and Savior, you can now make the choice to obtain your wealth inheritance by operating the principles that give you access to *"Spirit - Led Wealth."* The Holy Spirit is willing to be your guide but you have to make the choice.

"Somebody's Life Depends on You!"

CHAPTER 12

SPIRITUAL PRINCIPLES FOR A PERPETUAL HARVEST

The house of the righteous has great wealth, but trouble accompanies the income of the wicked. (Prov. 15:6).

The Word of God declares that there is great wealth in the house of the righteous and the income of the wicked is troubled. Considering the fact that the Scriptures cannot lie I must accept the above verse as the truth—although in the natural it seems inaccurate in the case of many of the righteous. Solomon who was the wisest man that ever lived penned Psalm 15:6, because during His time, wealth and riches was the rule and not the exception for the children of Israel.

Today, many of the righteous have squandered their treasure of wealth in exchange for debt. Like Adam and Eve, many have turned their dominion, power and prosperity over to the enemy through ignorance. The tragedy is, the world's point of view is received and believed more than the Word of God's viewpoint concerning money. I was astonished to see how many people lined up in the cold, at two and three o'clock in the morning, for the black Friday sales after Thanksgiving. As I watched the news I could not help but think, "What if people were this excited about funding the Kingdom of God." Pastor's and leader's, just think what it would be like to make a special appeal to fund ministry and then have to call in security to control the crowds. I believe the day is coming soon—through the teaching contained in this book and the many others like it. Until then, I want to give you some practical keys for increasing and managing your harvest.

The Lord gave me a prophetic word for you and it is this, "If you do not become debt-free in the spirit realm first—you will never be able manifest debt freedom in the natural realm." Secondly, "If you do not become wealthy inwardly there will be no wealth outwardly." The spiritual keys in this book have been designed to help you become wealthy inwardly so you can manifest wealth outwardly.

There are five keys that I want to leave you with that I personally exercise in my own life. These five keys have taken me from a state of bankruptcy (years ago) to a perpetual flow of increase and blessing in my life. I know that if you release your faith and put them into practice—you too will experience the perpetual flow of increase and blessing in your own life. The root of all five keys is *worship unto the Father*.

5 Spiritual Principles for a Perpetual Harvest:

Spiritual Principle 1: Keep God First through Worship. Reverence Him as Creator and Owner of Everything.

The truth is, you and I bought nothing into this world and surely we can take nothing out (see 1Timothy 6:7). God has left us as the manager's (steward's) of His property not the owners. *Worship* is what acknowledges and establishes God as the supreme authority in your life. Worship is an attitude of the heart —a heart that understands—God is the beginning and end of all things.

Give to the LORD, O families of the peoples, give to the Lord glory and strength. Give to the Lord the glory due His name; bring an offering, and come before Him. Oh, worship the LORD in the beauty of holiness (1 Chronicles 16:28-29 NKJV)!

"Stand up and bless the Lord your God forever and ever! *"Blessed be Your glorious name, which is exalted above all blessing and praise!* You alone are the Lord; You have made heaven, the heaven of heavens, with all their host, the earth and everything on it, the seas and all that is in them, and You preserve them all. The host of heaven worships You, (Nehemiah 9:5-6).

Spiritual Principle 2: Faithfully honor God with the first 10% (tithe) of all your income.

Tithing is a matter of trust and obedience. God gives the command to bring all the tithes into His storehouse in Malachi 3:10. The tithe that is consecrated unto the Lord establishes your trust in Him as your provider. God scolded the Israelites and accused them of robbing Him in the tithe. I often wondered, "How can a person rob God if He owns everything to begin with? The Holy Spirit then revealed to me that *the opportunity to bless His people* is what is robbed from God when they refuse to tithe. Disobeying God, by withholding the tithe, reveals a lack of trust in His ability to provide for you. If you refuse to tithe then you choose to be cursed. Remember: "The blessing of God cannot be released into a place that is cursed.

If you are not tithing you are robbing God of the opportunity to bless you. In Malachi 3:10, God promises to open the windows of heaven and pour out a blessing to the tither—that he will not have room enough to receive. Friend, tithing causes the blessing of God to rest upon everything you set your hands to do. Examine the description of the windows of heaven blessing from God as found in Deuteronomy 28:12:

The Lord will open to you His good treasure, *the heavens*, to give the rain to your land in its season, and *to **bless all the work of your hand. You shall lend to many nations**, but you shall not borrow.*

Tithing places God first as the provider and sustainer of your life. The windows of heaven are opened for God to prosper you when you trust Him with the tithe.

Spiritual Principle 3: Faithfully sow an offering (seed) above your tithe into Kingdom ministry.

There are a lot of people who believe they are sowing seed when they tithe. Tithing and sowing seed is not the same thing. The tithe is what opens the window of heaven—the seed you sow is what brings the blessing from heaven into your life. Too many people quit tithing because they do not see results—they fail to realize that they have no seed in the ground. There can be no harvest without a planted seed. Your tithe is given on the harvest (income) you have already received. The offering beyond the tithe is the seed that keeps a perpetual harvest coming.

While the earth remaineth, *seedtime and harvest*, and cold and heat, and summer and winter, and day and night shall not cease (Genesis 8:22 KJV).

And he said, so is the kingdom of God, *as if a man should cast seed into the ground*; and should sleep, and rise night and day, and *the seed should spring and grow up*, he knoweth not how. For the earth bringeth forth fruit of herself; first the blade, then the ear, after that the full corn in the ear. But when the fruit is brought forth, immediately he putteth in the sickle, *because the harvest is come* (Mark 4:26-29 KJV).

Give (sow), and it shall be given unto you; good measure, pressed down, and shaken together, and running over, *shall men give into your bosom.* For with the same measure that ye mete withal it shall be measured to you again, (Luke 6:38 KJV emphasis added).

The size of the seed you sow determines the size of the harvest you will grow. God's Word promises that when you sow to help others He will in turn help you.

Knowing that whatsoever good thing any man doeth, the same shall he receive of the Lord, whether he be bond or free, (Ephesians 6:8 KJV).

Be not deceived; God is not mocked: for whatsoever a man soweth, that shall he also reap, (Galatians 6:7).

Faithfully sowing seed into the Kingdom of God opens up doors and opportunities for people to use their power influence and ability to help you in your time of need.

Spiritual Key Four: Faithfully sow an *out of debt seed* into the life of the Prophet of God—Your Pastor.

The enemy has planted the lie in the Body of Christ that sound like this, "All those preachers want is your money." I use to believe that too; but thank God for revelation and deliverance. If the people of God truly embraced what you are about to learn here I am confident we will see a miraculous explosion of debt cancellation throughout the entire Body of Christ.

I want to show you through Scripture that there was a Prophet of God involved in every instance of debt cancellation.

1. 2 Kings 4:1-7- The widow woman's debt is cancelled through her obedience to the Prophet of God.

2. 2 Kings 6:1-7 – After calling to the Prophet of God for help a young man recovers a lost axe head that he had *borrowed.*

3. 1 Kings 17:10-16 – A woman receives relief and provision in the midst of a famine—after she obeyed the Prophet of God. The woman had set her heart that she and her son were going to eat their last cake and die. Her obedience in baking the Prophet of God a cake *first* resulted in her having provision throughout the famine with plenty left over. God is a keeper!

4. Nehemiah 5:1-13 – In this passage, Nehemiah is in the process of a building project on behalf of God—he turns to the people for an offering and they are all in debt to the point that their children had been sold into slavery. Nehemiah (the man of God) responded by going to the peoples creditors and asking them to cancel the debts. Guess what happened? The creditor's cancelled all of the debt! Read the record for yourself.

5. Matthew 17:25-27 – Jesus demonstrates that debt can be cancelled supernaturally, when He canceled the temple tax owed for Peter and Himself.

Money in the mouth of a fish is definitely *supernatural debt cancellation. This proves money is everywhere!*

6. Acts 4:32-35 – In this New Testament account of Scripture the people were so excited about the Gospel of Christ that they sold their possessions and laid the money at to Apostles feet. The result: **"Nor was there anyone among them who lacked; for all** who were possessors of lands or houses sold them, and **brought the proceeds of the things that were sold, and laid them at the apostles' feet;** and they distributed to each as anyone had need.

Okay, I think you have enough confirmation that supernatural debt cancellation is connected to obedience to the Prophet (Spiritual Leader) of God.

Next, I want to show you the principle of sowing into the lives of Spiritual Leaders.

1. 2 Chronicles 20:20 – Believe in the Lord your God, so shall you be established; believe his prophets so shall you *prosper.*

2. Matthew 10:41- "He that receives a prophet in the name of a prophet shall receive a prophets reward.

3. Galatians 6:6 – The one who is taught the message must share his goods with the teacher (HSCB).

4. 1 Corinthians 9:11-12, 14 – Paul teaches that those who preach the Gospel are to earn their living from the Gospel. The teaching that your pastor sows into your life is eternal while the gift you sow into his/her life is temporal.

5. Philippians 4:14-19 – Sowing into the life of your pastor opens up a debit and credit account in heaven. When you partner with your Pastor—God partners with you. Paul made it clear that the gift was well pleasing to God. You become a partaker of the anointing and blessing that flows upon your spiritual leader through the seed you sow.

Surely the Lord GOD does nothing, unless He reveals His secret to His servants the prophets (Amos 3:7).

I know I spent a lot of time on this particular key and it is because it is the most neglected one. You are overcoming the deceptions of the enemy and in order to do that you must know and act in accordance with the truth. Our family practiced this principle and watched God eliminate hundreds of thousands of dollars of debt. All I can say is, "IT WORKS!"

Now, you need to get all of your debt together, set up an appointment to meet with your pastor, and take the debt and ask him/her to come into agreement with you that the debt is canceled in Jesus name. The next thing you need to do is to establish an amount that you are going to consistently sow into your pastor as a debt cancellation seed. Make sure you begin sowing immediately. Lastly, I want you to write and tell me about all of the great blessings that God pours into your life as a result.

Spiritual Principle 5: Praise your way to increase!

This key is short, sweet and to the point. Praise releases the increase!

Let the peoples praise You, O God; Let all the peoples praise You. Then the earth shall yield her increase; God, our own God, shall bless us. God shall bless us, and all the ends of the earth shall fear Him. (Psalms 67:5-7 NKJV)

Praise the Lord! Blessed is the man who fears the Lord, who delights greatly in His commandments. His descendants will be mighty on earth; the generation of the upright will be blessed. *Wealth and riches will be in his house, and his righteousness endures forever.*
(Psalms 112:1-3 NKJV)

Now, you are equipped with the "Spiritual Principles to Access Your Wealth Inheritance so you can begin acquiring "Spirit-Led Wealth."

FINAL THOUGHTS:

"And from the days of John the Baptist until now the kingdom of heaven suffers violence, and the violent take it by force," (Matthew 11:12).

The goal of *"Spirit Led Wealth,"* is to provide you and every born again believer with the *"Spiritual Keys to Access Your Spiritual Inheritance!"* The intent of my heart in this writing this foundational book was to teach about wealth from God's perspective. I pray both my goal and intent have been expressed with clarity.

The Kingdom of God is suffering violence because the wealth of the righteous is consumed by the world's system of debt—this is not the will of God. The wealth transfer that everybody is waiting for begins when you make a conscious effort to transfer your money from the realm of debt—back into the kingdom of God. Secondly, the wealth transfer occurs every time a soul is saved. The new convert and his wealth; are transferred from the kingdom of darkness into the kingdom of Christ.

The enemy is advancing his kingdom of darkness with the wealth of the righteous—while the Kingdom of God suffers.   There are far too many Christians squandering their inheritance.   They have either been blinded by the lies of the enemy or they simply do not know how to properly steward the resources of God. This is why I desperately need your help in reaching as You ought to shout to the top of your lungs, "I am a Kingdom Heir!"   Now, declare that again, "I am a Kingdom Heir!"   That's right!   I stand in faith and declare to you right now, that as a *Kingdom Heir* of God in the spirit realm—you will also become the possessor of wealth in the earth realm.   Jesus Christ has canceled all of your debt and you are not waiting to become—you already are! The choice is yours!

Today, our heavenly Father is ready to pour wealth into the hands of those who will commit to advancing His Kingdom in the earth.   Our call is to reach lost souls with the gospel of Jesus Christ beginning with our family first.   Wealth without God at the center is equal to greed.   Here we are talking about "Spirit-Led Wealth," which is wealth acquired and directed by the leading of the Holy Spirit.

"Of what use is money in the hand of a [self-confident] fool to buy skillful and godly wisdom – when he has no understanding or heart for it?
(Proverbs 17:16 AMP)

There are many who have amassed wealth without acknowledging God as their source but when you look beyond the wealth you will find their lives are broken and without peace. *"Spirit-Led Wealth"* is internal oneness and peace with God first, which, shows up externally through manifested prosperity in every area of life. Let the be the beginning of allowing the Holy Spirit to guide you into your wealthy place in Christ!

Empowered To Prosper Faith Confessions

The Journey to Your Wealthy Place

...But You bought us to a wealthy place.   Psalms 66:12

The thief does not come except to steal, and to kill, and to destroy. I have come that they may have life,

and that they may have it more abundantly. John 10:10

Since you chose to purchase this book it is my guess that you are interested in living a life of abundance. No matter what your age or current status this book can be a major catalyst in changing the rest of your life. My desire is to instruct you in some timeless principles and promises from the Word of God that will strengthen your relationship with Him, reveal His heart to you and release you to fulfill your prophetic destiny. God wants you to be a millionaire so that His purposes can be fulfilled in the earth realm. God is looking for distribution centers, people that he can trust to obey him in the management and distribution of his wealth for kingdom purposes in the earth. Will you be the next Kingdom Millionaire? If so, you can begin confessing abundance into your life today.

This is a book of meditations and confessions along with a practical guide to bringing your financial affairs into alignment with God's will, that are designed for you to reflect upon and then act upon. It's time to challenge your belief system, unclog your heart, receive the Word of God and come in agreement with His will for your abundant life. Jesus clearly expressed that His purpose for coming to the earth was to give us life and an abundant life at that. Jesus was not only referring to the eternal life one receives upon accepting Him but a life complete in Him filled with love, joy, peace and happiness. God's will is that we walk in abundance in every area of our lives and this book is the beginning of your journey to your wealthy place in His kingdom.

Find a quiet place where you can sit, relax, and reflect on the confessions and meditations. Meditation simply means to reflect upon or think intently, to play over and over again. Confession means to declare or acknowledge your faith. Next record the revelation you receive. Listen for the voice of God to speak to you and then write down what you learned or the instructions you see in the passages of scripture. My prayer for you is that by the end of this book you will have a revelation of God's will for your abundant life, a heart motivated to bless the kingdom of God, and a mind ready to confess those things that be not in your life as they should be. As you commit to meditating and confessing the Word of God you will soon begin to see the blessings of God manifesting in your life like never before. You are a millionaire in manifestation. Let's begin the Journey to Your Wealthy Place!

COURAGE TO LEAP INTO ABUNDANCE

For God hath not given us the spirit of fear; but of power and of love, and of a sound mind. 2 Timothy 1:7

DAY 1

EMPOWERED TO PROSPER MEDITATION

Everyone dreams of being wealthy. Some go forth and make the dream into reality while others resign to fear and still others just give up and quit dreaming. Wealth was not created for just a select few. God is a God of abundance therefore there is no lack in Him. If there is no lack in Him then there should be no lack in those

He created. How can lack come out of abundance? God created you in His image and likeness and breathed into you His abundance and you became a living soul (speaking spirit). You were created and filled with abundance. Imagine what it would be like for a wealthy father to create a child and place him out in the world without any provision and protection for his well-being. Everyone would agree that only a cruel uncaring father could do such a thing. Well, God is a loving and giving Father who desires only the best for you. He wants a loving relationship with you and He invites you to come boldly to the throne of grace where you will find His mercy and unmerited favor. Don't be afraid, God wants you to be wealthy and so do I. Take a moment and meditate on your wealthy place. Where are you? What type of home do you have? What are you driving? Imagine no debt and a bank account that you can't count. God has blessed us with the incredible ability to meditate or imagine and then create what we see in our mind. This book began in my imagination then I created it and now you are reading it. Now imagine yourself with the courage to leap into God's abundance. Now Leap!

Let us therefore come boldly to the throne of grace that we may find mercy and grace to

help in the time of need. Hebrews 4:7

Empowered to Prosper   Faith Confession

I am created in the likeness and image of God who has breathed His abundance into me and made me to be a living soul, full of His abundance. I came from God who is abundance therefore there is no lack in my life. I am walking in power, love and a sound mind. I am enjoying the abundance of God's love and provision for me right now!

Day 2

CHOOSE THIS DAY: TO LIVE, PROSPER OR DIE!

See I set before you today life and prosperity, death and destruction. For I command you today to love the Lord your God, to walk in his ways, and to keep his commandments, decrees and laws; then you will live and increase, and the Lord your God will bless you in the land your are entering to possess. Deuteronomy 30:15

Now choose life, so that you and your children may live...Deuteronomy 30:19

EMPOWERED TO PROSPER MEDITATION

Today my friend you must make a choice between living a mediocre unfulfilled life and passing that curse to your children or living an abundant and prosperous life and passing that blessing to your children. Do you want to be a prosperous heir in the kingdom or a broke heir? God loves us so much that he has given us a plan to ensure our prosperity, but the choice is yours. God didn't say go to college, earn a degree, work two jobs, scrimp and save, invest in the right stocks and then you will increase. No! He simply said love him, do things according to his plan, and obey him, then you will live, increase and be blessed. God is abundance and in order for you to walk in your wealthy place you must come in agreement with His will. You have a choice to switch from the worlds plan that leads to death and destruction and choose God's plan of long life and prosperity. Your choice is not only about you but your children and the many generations that will come behind you. Break the curse of lack in your life today so that you and your seed may live and prosper. Choose to love God and follow Him. Now see yourself prosperous.

Know therefore that the Lord thy God, he is God, the faithful God, which keepeth covenant and mercy with them that love him and keep his commandments to a thousand generations...Deuteronomy 7:9

EMPOWERED TO PROSPER

I choose life and prosperity according to God's plan. I am living a life of prosperity and blessing. I am transferring life and prosperity to my children and they too live a wealthy and abundant life. I decree the blessing of prosperity and increase upon my seed for a thousand generations in Jesus name. Amen!

Day 3

HEIRS OF LIFE MORE ABUNDANTLY

The thief does not come except to steal, and to kill, and to destroy. I have come that they may have life, and that they may have it more abundantly. John 10:10

EMPOWERED TO PROSPER MEDITATION

I don't know about you my friend but today's scripture lets me know two very important things. First, Jesus Christ did not come to the earth and die for our sins just so we could get a ticket stamped heaven, No! He came that we may have life and not just an ordinary life but abundant life. This means that Jesus prepared the way for every believer not to just gain eternal life but to be able to live it abundantly which means in total fulfillment. Are you getting it in your spirit that there is no lack in the kingdom of God? Secondly, you can see the true culprit behind the lack and brokenness that may be manifested in your life. It's the devil himself! Satan plants the lies in your mind that you're not worthy of wealth, that serving God is being poor, or that you don't have the ability to create wealth in your life. Shout with a loud voice, "The devil is a liar!" Lift up your hands, your voice and your head with a resounding praise and step into the, Life More Abundantly," in Christ Jesus.

EMPOWERED TO PROSPER FAITH CONFESSION

I confess Christ Jesus as Lord and Saviour of my life. Jesus came that I might have life and have it more abundantly therefore, I accept "Life More Abundantly," into my spirit, soul and body right now and from this day forward. Lack is not my inheritance in Christ so I refuse to walk in less than "Life More Abundantly." God is abundance who gave me the gift of abundance through His Son Jesus Christ and I receive His free gift now in Jesus Name. Amen!

Day 4

DESTINED TO REIGN IN LIFE

For if by the one man's offense death reigned through the one, much more those who receive abundance of grace and of the gift of righteousness will reign in life through the One, Jesus Christ. (Romans 5:17)

EMPOWERED TO PROSPER MEDITATION

Yesterday we learned that Jesus came for the purpose of delivering the gift of "Life More Abundantly," to those who believe in Him. Well, today's verse allows you to see that the purpose for Jesus giving you entrance into "Life More Abundantly," is so you and I can "Reign" in this life. To reign means to occupy a throne with royal rule, authority and influence. Ephesians 2:6 declares that we have been raised up and made to sit together in the heavenly places in Christ Jesus. This is so powerful. You are not bound to the elements or circumstances of this world because Jesus Christ has restored you back to your original position of dominion and authority in the heavenly places. You are seated in heavenly places in Christ Jesus! This means you have the ability to call those things that be not as though they should be, Abundant! There is no lack, bad health, broken promises or bad neighborhoods in heaven which means they should not be manifest in your life here on earth. Break Free from the lack mindset today!

EMPOWERED TO PROSPER FAITH CONFESSION

I confess with my mouth and believe in my heart that I reign in this life through Christ Jesus and no weapon formed against me shall prosper. I walk in kingdom authority and power and I am seated in heavenly places in Christ therefore I speak to those things in my life that are not in agreement with God's best for my life and I command them to go now in Jesus name. I command lack to go, sickness and disease must go, the spirit of poverty must go, debt must go and I command everything in my life to line up and come in agreement with the will of God for my life now in Jesus name. I reign in this life through Christ Jesus, therefore I have dominion, authority, power and influence to change the world in which I live for God's glory.

Day 5

A CHOSEN GENERATION

But you are a chosen generation, a royal priesthood, a holy nation, His own special people, that you may proclaim the praises of Him who called you out of darkness into His marvelous light;

(1 Peter 2:9)

...and from Jesus Christ, the faithful witness, the firstborn from the dead, and the ruler over the kings of the earth. To Him who loved us and washed us from our sins in His own blood, and has made us kings and priests to His God and Father, to Him be glory and dominion forever and ever. Amen. (Revelation 1:5, 6)

EMPOWERED TO PROSPER MEDITATION

Five is considered the number of Grace. Grace is unmerited favor bestowed upon someone without them working or earning it in anyway. You can also think of Grace as: God's Riches At Christ's Expense. The world in which we live teaches us that we have to matriculate from certain universities or work, work, work, in order to earn something. However, in today's verses we learn that we are chosen, royalty, holy and God's own special people. We also learn that we are loved and have been made, "Kings and Priests," to God the Father by the blood of Christ. Isn't that great news! You are chosen to live in abundance. Have you ever seen a broke king or queen? So why have you allowed the enemy to tell you that you don't deserve to live a prosperous and wealthy life? God wouldn't give you dominion with no status. The problem is we've been conditioned to earn our status but God freely gives us all things to enjoy. When you accepted Christ you were translated out of darkness (the devils domain) into the kingdom of Christ (God's Domain) and just as Christ was crowned king so were you. He is King of Kings which means He's King of the Kings who are submitted to His lordship. He bestowed this abundant grace upon us out of His great love and nothing else. The king's responsibility was to decree laws and govern what could and could not enter a territory. So that means you have the power to decree a thing and it must come to pass. The key is we must decree (loose) those things that are lawful in heaven and bind those things that are not. Today begin binding debt, lack and sickness and loose health, wealth and prosperity in Jesus name. Remember: "You have not because you ask not. See yourself the way God sees you and begin creating your wealth today.

EMPOWERED TO PROSPER FAITH ONFESSION

I am a king of the most High King and as such I have the authority to decree a thing and it shall come to pass. I decree that I am wealthy; all of my needs are met; all of my relationships prosper and I have favor with both God and man. People use their power, influence and ability to help me because I use my influence to help others. I decree that I reign as king and priest and I shall show forth the praises of God all the days of my life. There is no lack in my life. I am blessed, blessed, blessed, abundantly blessed!

Day 6

WEALTH WITH A KINGDOM MISSION

Father, I remember today that it is You, the Lord my God who is continually giving me power and ability to get wealth that your covenant may be confirmed on the earth. Deuteronomy 8:18

EMPOWERED TO PROSPER MEDITATION

How much better can life be? God has not only given us status as kings and priests but He has also given us the ability to get (create) wealth. Anyone who knows God also knows that He never does anything without a purpose. Today we discover that the whole purpose of this wealth business is for the purpose of continuing

God's covenant in the earth. You see friend when Jesus left the earth He didn't leave us without strength but He sent the Holy Spirit as a gift to empower us to be His witnesses in the earth (Acts 1:8). So the purpose for our wealth is to spread the good news of Jesus Christ and meet the spiritual needs of His people here in the earth. Yes! God wants you to represent Him as an ambassador to the lost so they too can enjoy eternal life and the kingdom privilege of "Life More Abundantly." Wealth and prosperity has to be about souls otherwise we are gathering uncertain riches. Uncertain riches means your money doesn't have a divine mission to serve the kingdom of God therefore as easy as it comes it goes. Haggai 1:7-8 testifies to this fact. The Lord said, "You looked for much but it came to little; and when you brought it home I blew it away." God is revealing to us that when our wealth is not serving kingdom purposes as it was intended to then it will fly away just as fast as it comes in. Commit to aligning yourself with God's kingdom mission and watch as abundance begins to flow to you freely and effortlessly.

EMPOWERED TO PROSPER FAITH CONFESSION

I confess that I am a money magnet. Money is attracted to me because I have a kingdom agenda. I serve the kingdom of God with my money. I am a channel and the blessings of God flow through me. My abundance is making everyone better off. Souls are being saved, delivered and set free because my abundance makes it possible for the Gospel to be preached around the world. I live an abundant, prosperous life that's full of growing, sharing, and serving. It's great to live in abundance for abundance is my natural state.

Day 7

THE ANOINTING FOR ABUNDANCE RELEASED

Jesus, I thank you for your grace, for though you were rich you became poor, that I through your poverty might become rich. (2 Corinthians 8:9)

Christ has redeemed me from the curse of the law, being made a curse for me so that the blessing of Abraham might come on me (Galatians 3:13-14)

EMPOWERED TO PROSPER MEDITATION

Dearly beloved we have made it to day seven and seven is the number of completion. I believe that if you have made it this far then there is nothing on earth that can prevent you from walking in your wealthy place. Our scripture focus reveals to us that Jesus did not just come and die for our sins but he broke every curse of the enemy. That means you and I are free to be healthy, wealthy and prosperous. When we speak the name of Jesus we are actually referring to the Anointed One and His Anointing. When Jesus became poor so that we might be made rich He imparted to us an anointing to prosper. Do you see it? You have an anointing to destroy lack and create wealth. So what's preventing you from believing God for a first class lifestyle? As we close our week of meditation I want you to remember that everyday is filled with choices. Nobody has the power to make choices for you; you are responsible for your choices. When you book a flight they ask you do you want to fly coach or first class and I believe life asks us this question every day. From this day forward every time you make a choice remember that Royalty always goes "First Class." Begin to look and seek first class opportunities. Live from your spiritual state of abundance and not the natural state of circumstances. You are not waiting to become you already are everything you can imagine in Christ Jesus. Celebrate you are in your wealthy place right now. Visualize it and embrace it. It's yours!

EMPOWERED TO PROSPER FAITH CONFESSION

I am a faithful tither because I love God and His kingdom; The devourer is rebuked from my life and the fruit of my ground is prosperous; my vine shall bear fruit in season; I honor the Lord from my wealth and from the first of all my produce, and my barns are filled with plenty and my vats are overflowing...I am diligent in all my work and I am made rich...I thank You Father that it is Your blessing that makes me rich and no sorrow comes with it...Father, I thank you that as I sow I will increase all the more...I am a generous man and I prosper in all that I set my hand to do, I water others and I too will be watered...thank you that adversity pursues sinners, but I, a righteous man, am rewarded with prosperity...I call forth the wealth of the sinner into my life, for it is stored up for me...I leave an inheritance to my children's children and the blessing of prosperity flows through my bloodline for a thousand generations. Malachi 3:8-17; Proverbs 3:9; 10:4, 22; 11:24, 25; 13 21, 22

Day 8

THE SEASON OF NEW BEGINNINGS

 Bless the Lord, you His angels, who excel in strength, who do his Word, heeding the voice of His Word. Bless the Lord, all you His hosts, you ministers of his, who do His pleasure. Bless the Lord, all His works, in all places of His dominion. Bless the Lord, O my soul. (Psalms 103:20-22)

Go ahead and declare: Today is the first day of the best days of my life. I have a new mind concerning wealth and I will confess my prosperity from this day forward. Well friend this is the official day of "New Beginnings." Following is a list of faith scriptures so that you can activate heavens best to come forth in your life. The angels of the Lord are given as your ministers for the purpose of bringing the Word of God to pass in your life. Do you realize that this means you have a whole army of angels ready to go to work and bring heavens best into your life? The Angels are standing by ready to hearken to the Word of the Lord and then they go and bring forth whatever His Word commands. The beautiful thing about this is you have authority to speak the Word of God with boldness and when you speak the Word of God the Angels respond to you just like they respond to Father God. Now that's what I call awesome. Our heavenly Father has given us everything we need to create the most abundant life we could ever live. Think about it you created where you are right now based on the words you spoke. So if you don't like where you are and you're ready to breakthrough to your wealthy place start opening your mouth and speaking what the Word of God says you can be, do and have in Jesus name!

Your Tithe is the Covenant Connection to "Life More Abundantly." When you become faithful with the tithe then God knows He can trust you to handle His true riches. The offering is your seed. Genesis 8:22 instructs us that as long as the earth remains the principle of seed, time and harvest will never cease. That means for every seed you plant you can rightly expect a harvest. Now it's important to understand that the tithe is what opens the heavens to rain on your offerings (seed) so that you receive a harvest from your sowing. If you are not tithing then you're walking under a closed heaven therefore even though you may give; you won't receive the maximum return on your gift because there is no rain to water your seed. Tithing connects you to the promises of God and assures that you have heavens backing on all of your financial endeavors. After all Malachi 3:8 tells us that we rob God of the opportunity to bless and prosper us and place ourselves under a curse when we don't tithe. So the bottom line is if you want your confessions to produce results make sure you're connected through tithing and then plant your seeds into good ground and watch your harvest grow!

I have listed scripture confessions to help you activate your faith and bring your wealth from the spiritual realm (Ephesians 1:3) into the physical realm. As you speak the Word of God you are not attempting to make something happen but you are actually speaking the truth of God's Word and causing His prepared blessing to be released to you. Everything you need is in the spiritual realm and you cause it to manifest through your confession of faith. Open your mouth wide a water your seed with your daily confession.

WEALTH BUIDLING CONFESSION OF FAITH

"Thou hast crowned my year with Your goodness and all of my paths drip with abundance".

(Psalm 65:11)

I seek the Lord, so I will not lack any good thing (Psalm 34:10).

I seek first the kingdom of God and His righteousness, so all these things will be added to me (Matthew 6:33).

I will remember the Lord my God, for it is He who gives me power to get wealth so that He may establish His covenant that He swore to my forefathers (Deuteronomy 8:18).

I obey and serve God, so I will spend my days in prosperity, and my years in pleasures (Job 36:11).

God has given to me all things that pertain to life and godliness, through the knowledge of Him who has called me to glory and virtue (2 Peter 1:3).

This book of the law will not depart out of my mouth, but I will meditate on it day and night, that I may observe to do according to all that is written in it. For then God will make my way prosperous, and then I will have good success (Joshua 1:8).

The Lord my God teaches me to profit, and leads me in the way that I should go (Isaiah 48:17).

The Lord desires above all things that I may prosper and be in health, even as my soul prospers

(3 John 2)

The Lord has pleasure in my prosperity, since I am His servant (Psalm 35:27).

God will go before me and make the crooked places straight. He will break the gates of brass in pieces, and cut the bars of iron in two. And He will give me the treasures of darkness, and hidden riches of secret places (Isaiah 45:2-3).

The Lord will open to me His good treasure—the heavens to give rain to my land in His season, and to bless all the work of my hands; and I will lend to many nations, and I will not borrow. The Lord will make me the head, and not the tail; and I will be above only, and I will not be beneath if I listen to the commandments of the Lord my God, to observe and to do them (Deuteronomy 28:12-13).

My God will supply all my needs according to His riches in glory by Christ Jesus (Philippians 4:19).

He who did not spare His own Son, but delivered Him up for us all, will also freely give me all things (Romans 8:32).

Christ has redeemed me from the curse of the law, being made a curse for me so that the blessing of Abraham might come on me (Galatians 3:13-14).

Jesus is my mediator of a better covenant, which was established upon better promises

(Hebrews 8:6).

know the grace of my Lord Jesus Christ, that He was rich, yet for my sake He became poor so that I, through His poverty, might be rich (2 Corinthians 8:9).

The blessings of the Lord make me rich, and He adds no sorrow to them (Proverbs 10:22).

I do not fear, for it is my Father's good pleasure to give me the kingdom (Luke 12:32).

I am willing and obedient, so I will eat the good of the land (Isaiah 1:19).

I obey and serve God, so I will spend my days in prosperity, and my years in pleasures (Job 36:11).

I am faithful, so I will abound with blessings (Proverbs 28:20).

I delight in the Lord, and He will give me the desires of my heart (Psalm 37:4).

I give, and it will be given to me. Good measure, pressed down, shaken together, and running over, will men give to me (Luke 6:38).

I am not slothful, but I am a follower of those who through faith and patience inherit the promises (Hebrews 6:12).

I do not grow weary in doing good; therefore, in due season I will reap, if I do not give up (Galatians 6:9).

God is doing exceedingly abundantly above all that I ask or think, according to the power that works in me (Ephesians 3:20).

The wealth of the sinner is laid up for me, the righteous and I leave an inheritance to my children's children (Proverbs 13:22).

Wealth and riches are in my house because I am empowered with god's anointing and favor to draw wealth. (Psalms 112:3; Deuteronomy 8:18)

God's favor brings promotion and causes me to increase daily (Esther 2:17; Psalms 75:6-7)

The Lord loads me daily with His benefits, I am the righteousness of God in Christ Jesus and I flourish in the courts of my Lord (Psalms 68:19; 92:13)

I will not fear for the Lord will contend with those that contend with me; and He will always bring me into a place of abundance. (Isaiah 41:10; Psalms 66:12)

ENJOY YOUR WEALTHY PLACE!

Spirit-Led Wealth

Spiritual Principles to Access Your

Wealth Inheritance

This is the foundational book of the "Spirit-Led Wealth" Series

To Order Additional Copies or for Event Booking

Contact: spiritledwealth@gmail.com or visit
www.sonyahamm.com.

CPSIA information can be obtained
at www.ICGtesting.com
Printed in the USA
FSOW03n0912050716
22360FS

9 781532 723971